National 5 ENGLISH
READING FOR UNDERSTANDING, ANALYSIS AND EVALUATION

Mary M. Firth and Andrew G. Ralston

HODDER
EDUCATION
AN HACHETTE UK COMPANY

The authors would like to thank Lara Bradley and Veronica Reece of Hutchesons' Grammar School, Glasgow, for their valuable contributions to this book.

The Publishers would like to thank the following for permission to reproduce copyright material:

Photo credits: See page 98.

Acknowledgements: John Armstrong: page 21, extract from *The Secret Power of Beauty (Penguin Books, 2004);* **Mark Arnold-Forster:** pages 57–58, extract from *The World at War (William Collins/Fontana Books/Thames TV, 1976);* **Bill Bryson:** pages 5–6, extract from *Down Under (Black Swan, 2001);* **Dave Calhoun:** pages 32–34, Daniel Craig interview in *Time Out (Monday October 27, 2008), reproduced by permission of the publisher;* **Agatha Christie:** page 17, extract from *Dumb Witness (HarperCollins, 2008);* **Peter Clayton:** pages 42–44, 'The interview'; text and images from *Body Language at Work: Read the Signs & Make the Right Moves (Hamlyn, 2003), copyright © Peter Clayton and Duncan Petersen Publishing Ltd 2003, reproduced by permission of The Octopus Publishing Group;* **Ray Connolly:** pages 83–84, 'End of the line', abridged and adapted from the *Daily Mail (20 August 2012), reproduced by permission of Solo Syndication;* **David Derbyshire:** pages 78–79, 'Time to ration your rashers!', adapted and abridged from the *Daily Mail (20 August 2012), reproduced by permission of Solo Syndication;* **Anne Donovan:** page 22, extract from *Buddha Da (Canongate Books, 2009);* **Jean Faley:** pages 37–38, extract from *Up Oor Close: Memories of Domestic Life in Glasgow Tenements, 1901–1945 (White Cockade Publishing, 1990), reproduced by permission of the author;* **Gordon Ferris:** page 11, extract from *Bitter Water (Corvus, 2012), copyright © Gordon Ferris 2012, reproduced by permission of Atlantic Books;* **Nigel Jones:** pages 49–51, 'Houses of HORROR' from *Weekend Magazine (11 August 2012), reproduced by permission of Solo Syndication on behalf of the Daily Mail;* **Victor Klemperer:** page 20, extracts adapted and abridged from *To the Bitter End: The Diaries of Victor Klemperer,* translated by Martin Chalmers (Phoenix, 2000), translation © Martin Chalmers 1999, reproduced by permission of The Orion Publishing Group, London;* **Alistair MacLean:** pages 58–59, extract adapted and abridged from *HMS Ulysses (Collins/Sterling, 2011), reprinted by permission of HarperCollins Publishers Ltd;* **John MacLeod:** pages 80–81, 'Goodbye, and thanks for all those fine and Dandy memories', adapted from the *Daily Mail (16 August 2012), reproduced by permission of Solo Syndication;* **Christopher Middleton:** pages 86–87, 'I've got an incurable hoarder disorder' from the *Daily Telegraph (8 August 2012), © Telegraph Media Group Limited 2012, reproduced by permission of Telegraph Media Group Limited;* **Paul Hudson** and **David Millward:** pages 25–28, '80mph speed limit: The arguments for and against' from the *Daily Telegraph (13 October 2011), © Telegraph Media Group Limited 2011, reproduced by permission of Telegraphy Media Group Limited;* **Peter Morwood:** page 20, extract from *The Demon Lord (Arrow Books, 1986), © 1984 Arrow Books;* **George Orwell:** page 18, extract from 'Shooting an Elephant' from *Inside the Whale and Other Essays (Penguin Books, 1969);* **T.C. Smout:** page 21, extract adapted and abridged from *A History of the Scottish People 1560-1830 (William Collins, 1969);* **Aileen Duffy, Richard Cherrie** and **Gail Staddon:** pages 17–18, extract from *Psychology for Higher: The Textbook for Psychology (Unity Publications, 2005), © Unity Publications 2005, reproduced by permission of the publisher;* **Alan Taylor:** pages 74–75, 'Scotland needs to clean up its tourism', adapted from pages 17–18 the *Herald (March, 2012), reproduced with kind permission of the Herald & Times Group;* **Claire Tomalin:** pages 69–70, extract adapted from *Jane Austen, A Life (Viking, 1997), reproduced by permission of Penguin Books;* **Sally Williams:** pages 76–77, 'School's out: how Britain embraced the junior prom', condensed from the *Telegraph Magazine (11 August 2012), reproduced by permission of Telegraph Media Group Limited;* **Jacqueline Wilson:** pages 64–65, 'Jacqueline Wilson's childhood picnics' from the *Daily Telegraph (1 August 2012), © Telegraph Media Group Limited 2012, reproduced by permission of Telegraph Media Group Limited;* **Benjamin Zephaniah:** page 40, extract from 'I love me mudder' from *The Dread Affair: Collected Poems (Arena Arrow Books, 1985).*

Every effort has been made to trace all copyright holders, but if any have been inadvertently overlooked the Publishers will be pleased to make the necessary arrangements at the first opportunity.

Although every effort has been made to ensure that website addresses are correct at time of going to press, Hodder Gibson cannot be held responsible for the content of any website mentioned in this book. It is sometimes possible to find a relocated web page by typing in the address of the home page for a website in the URL window of your browser.

Hachette UK's policy is to use papers that are natural, renewable and recyclable products and made from wood grown in sustainable forests. The logging and manufacturing processes are expected to conform to the environmental regulations of the country of origin.

Orders: please contact Bookpoint Ltd, 130 Park Drive, Abingdon, Oxon OX14 4SE. Telephone: (44) 01235 827720. Fax: (44) 01235 400454. Lines are open 9.00–5.00, Monday to Saturday, with a 24-hour message answering service. Visit our website at **www.hoddereducation.co.uk**. Hodder Gibson can be contacted direct on: Tel: 0141 848 1609; Fax: 0141 889 6315; email: **hoddergibson@hodder.co.uk**

© Mary M Firth and Andrew G Ralston 2013

First published in 2013 by

Hodder Gibson, an imprint of Hodder Education,
An Hachette UK Company
2a Christie Street
Paisley PA1 1NB

Impression number   5 4 3 2 1

Year   2017 2016 2015 2014 2013

Cover photo © gyso4ka – Fotolia.com
Illustrations by Barking Dog Art
Typeset in 11 on 13.5 Helvetica Neue 45 Light by Integra Software Services Pvt. Ltd., Pondicherry, India
Printed in Spain

A catalogue record for this title is available from the British Library

ISBN: 978 1 4441 9208 7

Contents

Introduction

For the teacher

This book provides material for the implementation of Curriculum for Excellence in English. It is designed to assist in preparation for the Reading for Understanding, Analysis and Evaluation paper of the National 5 exam, which is worth 30 marks. These 30 marks will be awarded for addressing the challenge of applying reading skills in understanding, analysis and evaluation to one unseen text. Candidates will be assessed on answering questions that require them to show these reading skills and to complete tasks that involve inference making and summarising.

The book is centred around one of the key aspects of the National 5 course as defined in the Support Notes:

Tasks that encourage learners to understand key ideas and writer's attitude, analyse literary techniques (punctuation, sentence structure, imagery, tone) and evaluate the effectiveness of a text should be embedded in teaching methodology.

In addition to six practice papers closely modelled on the National 5 examination, the book provides a range of language activities designed to assist teachers with other aspects of the course, particularly the writing folio.

Special features

- In line with CfE thinking, a significant number of the follow-up tasks in the book will be suitable for oral work (talking and listening).
- Unlike other close reading books, several of the extracts are drawn from oral sources, e.g. an interview transcript and an extract from a book drawing on oral history sources.
- Each section of Part One of the book highlights various technical aspects of writing (structure, tone, use of language etc.) with follow-up tasks.
- Each section contains a 'Word game', i.e. a vocabulary-building exercise.
- Where appropriate, talk-based activities *('What do you think?')* and 'active learning' activities are included, e.g. students may be directed to research certain aspects on their own.
- A significant amount of source material is drawn from Scottish sources.
- At the end of each chapter in Part One there is a progress review summary box of 'I can ...' statements based on the topics covered.

All explanations and tasks in this book will relate to the aspects of language drawn from national guidelines listed below under the heading 'Using this book'.

For the student

The way education is delivered in schools has changed in recent years. Schools have been thinking more about the kind of skills young people need to succeed in life after leaving school. While you may not think so at times, there is a purpose to the activities you undertake during school time. Schools aim to educate young people to be:

- successful learners
- confident individuals

- responsible citizens
- effective contributors.

The purpose of this book is to show how your English lessons can be part of a process that helps you to achieve these four goals.

But how can, for example, studying a play by William Shakespeare or a poem by Robert Burns or answering questions on a close reading passage help you to become a 'responsible citizen' or an 'effective contributor'?

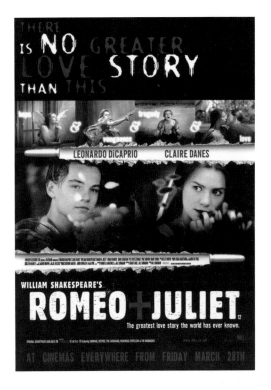

Studying such texts is relevant to everyday life. For example, themes and ideas in plays, poems or novels, whether they were written in the 1600s, 1800s or last year, deal with aspects of human life that do not change. Shakespeare's Macbeth is destroyed by his ruthless ambition and falls from grace. Burns' 'To a Mouse' deals with how humans treat animals. As such, they have something to say to us today. If you have seen the Leonardo DiCaprio and Claire Danes version of *Romeo and Juliet*, you will have seen how the themes of the play – love against the background of a feud – are exactly the same when the story is told in a modern American setting instead of a medieval Italian one.

In the same way, to be a 'confident individual' and an 'effective communicator' you need to have a good command of language, both in its written and spoken forms.

An obvious relevance of these skills to real life would be making a job application: if you cannot express yourself in a letter or email, or convey your skills in an interview, you are not likely to be offered the post.

These aims are kept in mind throughout this book. For example, many of the extracts are drawn from newspapers, as these not only demonstrate the skills of communication that everyone requires, but also deal with topical subjects that active citizens ought to think about and have opinions on. In this way, successful learners can become confident individuals who are able to participate fully in social, economic, cultural and even political life.

Again, to be an 'effective contributor' it is important not only to be able to think and work independently but to work in a collaborative way – in other words, with other people in a group, learning to share opinions, taking on board others' views and justifying your own. As a result, the tasks you will be asked to perform in this book include both writing for a variety of different purposes and talking, either individually or as part of a group discussion.

All these skills are known as 'transferable skills' – they are not simply of use in an English class. They overlap with the approaches being taken in other subject areas and equip you with the skills required beyond school.

This, then, is more than just another English textbook. Regard it as a tool that will enable you to become a successful learner, a confident individual, a responsible citizen and an effective contributor.

Assessment

While education has these broad aims, it also has to find ways of gauging how far you are progressing towards achieving them. This is why we have assessments and exams. The examination system has been changed to reflect the new priorities in education.

Following the new National 5 course will involve you in a number of different assessment tasks. The final assessment has two components:

- a **portfolio**, worth 30 marks, testing writing skills
- a **question paper**, worth 70 marks, testing reading skills

The question paper has two sections:

- **critical reading**, based on a study of prepared literature texts (40 marks)
- **reading for understanding, analysis and evaluation** (30 marks)

This book will help you to prepare for the second of these sections, 'reading for understanding, analysis and evaluation'. The 30 marks will be awarded for addressing the challenge of applying reading skills to one unseen text.

Assessment will involve answering questions to show these reading skills and completing a task that involves inference-making and summarising.

Using this book

In the course of working through this book, you should acquire the following skills:

- identifying the writer's **purpose** and the **genre** to which a piece of writing belongs
- distinguishing between the **main ideas** of the passage and the **supporting details and evidence** used to back these up
- **summarising** the writer's main points
- **drawing inferences** from what the writer says
- expanding the range of your **vocabulary**
- identifying how word patterns are determined by aspects of punctuation and sentence structure
- analysing the **structure and layout** of a passage, examining in particular how a writer uses **linking methods**
- understanding the appropriate literary terminology
- recognising the differences between **formal and informal registers** and distinguishing between **spoken and written forms** of expression
- **engaging with a text**, i.e. not simply understanding the content and analysing the style but conveying your feelings and reactions to these.

Part One looks at material from a variety of sources, which will help you to identify these features and develop the skills of working with them.

Part Two consists of passages with questions, which will help you apply the skills of understanding, analysis and evaluation by practising questions modelled on those in the National 5 exam papers.

While the book focuses on reading skills, there is much that will assist you in the writing part of the course as well. For example, the portfolio requires you to exhibit:

- skills in writing in different genres
- skills in writing for a range of purposes and audiences.

To acquire these skills, you need to understand what different genres and purposes are, and the way to do that is to see how professional writers approach their work.

Part One

Acquiring the skills

Chapter 1
Purpose
Four key questions

Why?

What?

How?

How effective?

In order to analyse a piece of writing successfully, you must consider four key questions. You must think about **what** the writer is saying; **how** he or she is saying it and then decide **how effective** the piece is. But first, it is important to decide **why** the author has written the piece.

Writing has many purposes. Below are ten of the main ones.

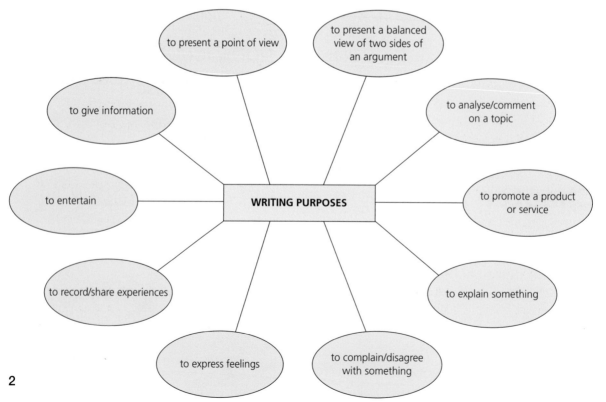

✎ *For practice*

On a wide sheet of paper, or a page turned sideways, draw a table with three columns. Copy the list of ten purposes from the spider diagram into the first column, one below the other. (Copying the purposes will help you to remember them.) In the second column, enter opposite the number of the example from the list below that you think best matches the purpose. (There is **one** example of each purpose.) Then, think of as many other examples as you can for each purpose and enter them in the third column.

1 An article debating the value of a university education compared with the advantages of going straight into work.

2 A newspaper report from a war zone.

3 An article detailing personal experience of treatment for cancer.

4 A newspaper article advocating reducing the voting age to sixteen.

5 A comic strip.

6 A letter to a newspaper objecting to cuts in social services for the elderly.

7 A magazine article on the star of a film that is about to be released.

8 A personal diary.

9 A leaflet accompanying a smartphone.

10 An article looking at the effect of texting on children's writing.

🔧 *Tools of the trade: register*

A writer will use a **register** that is appropriate to his or her purpose. The word '**register**' describes a form of language used in particular circumstances. Sentence structures and word choice make up a 'register'. For example, a piece of writing containing many Scottish words would be appropriate for a Scottish newspaper, but would be unlikely to appear in a paper read throughout the UK.

The register used for a professional textbook would include complex sentences and jargon words, whereas the register used for a book for toddlers would have very simple words and short sentences, and include the frequent use of repetition, which would be unacceptable in other forms of writing.

For some purposes, the register comprises formal, academic language, and for other purposes informal words and slang may be used.

Tone

One important aspect of register is **tone.** Tone refers to the manner in which a piece is written, and the attitude of the writer that this reveals. The tone of a piece of writing can be **personal** or **impersonal**.

If the tone is **personal**:

● The writer's personality and personal experience may come over strongly.

● The word 'I' is likely to occur frequently.

● The writer's thoughts and feelings will be expressed.

> 4 Main Street,
>
> Anytown
>
> 10 July
>
> Dear Julie,
>
> How are you? I just have to tell you about my holiday! What a disaster! I thought it would never end!

If the tone is **impersonal**:

● The piece will not reveal anything about the writer.

● The writing is likely to concentrate on facts and information.

● Ideas will be expressed without revealing the writer's own feelings.

> The Ming dynasty of China was established in 1368 by Chu Yuan Chang. It lasted until 1644 when it was superseded by the rule of the Manchus.

You must consider if the writer is being **serious**, or is subtly commenting on the subject by using **humour** or **irony**. Look for techniques such as:

- the **juxtaposing** (placing side by side) of **formal and informal** expression
- the use of sound effects such as **alliteration**.

Tone bank

If a question asks you to focus on **tone**, you could select one or more of the adjectives from the list below to describe the tone of the piece of writing.

angry questioning persuasive ironic
serious sarcastic humorous pleading
mock-serious disappointed playful
frightened resentful thoughtful shocked
tongue-in-cheek

💬 *For discussion*

'The last piece of chocolate cake'

In groups of two or three, select a tone from the tone bank. Without telling anyone what it is, say 'You ate the last piece of chocolate cake'. The others in the group should guess which tone you are using.

Readership

Closely tied in with writers' aims is the readership they have in mind. Most of the pieces you will be given to analyse will have been written for the non-specialist, general adult reader. But writing might also be directed at:

- small children
- teenagers
- members of a profession or people with expert knowledge
- people with special interest in a topic.

Writers adopt different styles and registers according to the readership they are aiming for, but will occasionally move into a different one to achieve a particular effect. For example, a writer might adopt a childish register to achieve a humorous or mocking effect.

A universal aim

Writers all have one universal aim – to be read! **All** writers aim to attract and hold their readers' attention, and you will be asked to analyse the tricks of the trade they use to achieve this.

✒ *For practice*

The following pieces of writing are written in different registers to fulfil different purposes. For each piece, explain:

a) the purpose of the piece
b) the intended readership
c) **two** or more features of the **register** used.

1 This Last Will & Testament is made by me, William James McDonald of 20 Park Road, Glasgow, G46 2PW. I revoke all previous wills and codicils. I appoint as executors and trustees of my will Peter William McDonald and Jennifer Rachel McDonald, both of 20 Park Road, Glasgow, G46 2PW.

2 Irish Sea: Southwesterly backing easterly 4 or 5, occasionally 6 later in south. Slight or moderate. Rain or showers. Good, occasionally poor.

Shannon: South 5 or 6, becoming cyclonic then northwest 5 to 7, perhaps gale 8 later. Moderate or rough, occasionally very rough later. Rain then squally showers. Good, occasionally poor.

3   The little pig built a house of sticks. Just after the house was finished, along came a wolf. He knocked at the door of the little pig's house and said, 'Little pig, little pig, let me come in.' The little pig answered, 'No, No, by the hair of my chinny chin chin, I'll not let you in.' Then the wolf said, 'Then I'll huff and I'll puff and I'll blow your house down.' So he huffed and he puffed until he blew the house down and he ate up the little pig.

4   My w/e wz CWOT Had 2 stay @ hm coz my bro n 3 aaah kdz wr dwn frm Ldn. LOL. Dd U C d nu Bond flm? Hurd its gr8.

5   Researchers in Germany have moved one step closer to closing the 'quantum metrology triangle', by fabricating a proof-of-principle circuit that links two quantum electrical devices in series, for the first time. A closed triangle – something scientists have been chasing for more than 20 years – would finally allow standardised units of voltage, current and resistance to be defined solely in terms of fundamental constants of nature.

Multipurpose writing

You may have noticed that many pieces of writing have more than one purpose. For example, war reporters in newspapers usually write impersonally and aim only to give information, but travel writers often choose a personal, humorous style, and aim to amuse their readers as much as to inform.

Writers of textbooks must instruct readers on a subject, but most try to present the material in an entertaining way. However, their *main* purpose is to give information, while entertaining the reader is a *secondary* purpose. One of your tasks will be to identify the writer's various purposes and rank them in this way.

The following exercise illustrates an example of writing that has more than one purpose.

◆   The extract below is taken from *Down Under*, an account of travelling through Australia by the American writer **Bill Bryson**. Read the extract, thinking first about the writer's purpose(s).

Canberra

1   You approach Canberra along a dual carriageway through rural woodland, which gradually morphs into a slightly more urban boulevard, though still in woodland, until finally you arrive at a zone of well-spaced but significant-looking buildings and you realize that you are there – or as near there as you can get in a place as scattered and vague as Canberra. It's a very strange city, in that it's not really a city at all, but rather an extremely large park with a city hidden in it. It's all lawns and trees and hedges and a big ornamental lake – all very agreeable, just a little unexpected.

2   I took a room in the Hotel Rex for no other reason than that I happened upon it and had never stayed in a hotel named for a family pet. The Hotel Rex was exactly what you would expect a large hotel built of concrete and called the Rex to be. But I didn't care. I was eager to stretch my legs and gambol about in all that green space. So I checked in, dumped my bags and returned at once to the open air. I'd passed a visitors' centre on the way in, and recollected it as being a short walk away, so I decided to start there. In the event, it was a long way – a very long way, as things in Canberra invariably prove to be.

3   The visitors' centre was almost ready to close when I got there, and in any case was just an outlet for leaflets and brochures for tourist attractions and places to stay. In a side room was a small cinema showing one of those desperately upbeat promotional films with a title like *Canberra – It's Got It All!* – the ones that boast how you can water ski and shop for an evening gown and have a pizza all in the same day because this place has … *got it all!* You know the kind I mean. But I watched the film happily because the room was air conditioned and it was a pleasure to sit after walking so far.

4 It was just as well that I didn't require an evening gown or a pizza or water skiing when I returned to the street because I couldn't find a thing anywhere. My one tip for you if you ever go to Canberra is don't leave your hotel without a good map, a compass, several days' provisions and a mobile phone with the number of a rescue service. I walked for two hours through green, pleasant, endlessly identical neighbourhoods, never entirely confident that I wasn't just going round in a large circle. From time to time I would come to a leafy roundabout with roads radiating off in various directions, each presenting an identical vista of antipodean suburban heaven, and I would venture down the one that looked most likely to take me to civilization only to emerge ten minutes later at another identical roundabout. I never saw another soul on foot or anyone watering a lawn or anything like that. Very occasionally a car would glide past, pausing at each intersection, the driver looking around with a despairing expression that said: 'Now where on earth is my house?'

⊕ Taking a closer look

In groups:

a) Discuss how many of the purposes listed on the diagram on page 2 this piece of writing fulfils. (You should be able to find at least five.)

b) Rank the purposes in order of importance.

Now copy the table below and look at the **quotations**. Each could be used as **evidence** that the piece fulfils a particular purpose. Decide what that purpose is. (Sometimes the example will illustrate more than one purpose.)

Quotation		Purpose
1	'You approach Canberra along a dual carriageway through rural woodland …'	
2	'… a place as scattered and vague as Canberra.'	
3	'… a hotel named for a family pet'	
4	'I was eager to stretch my legs and gambol about in all that green space.'	
5	'it was … a very long way, as things in Canberra invariably prove to be.'	
6	'… just an outlet for leaflets and brochures for tourist attractions and places to stay.'	
7	'… it was a pleasure to sit after walking so far.'	
8	'… don't leave your hotel without a good map, a compass, several days' provisions and a mobile phone with the number of a rescue service.'	
9	'… green, pleasant, endlessly identical neighbourhoods …'	
10	'I never saw another soul on foot or anyone watering a lawn or anything like that.'	

🔑 Focus on meaning

Now think about **what** the writer is saying.

1 Sum up the first impressions of Canberra that Bryson describes in the first paragraph, showing how he uses language to create a generally **positive** picture. Comment on

at least two **positive** words or expressions Bryson uses and explain their effect.

2 In paragraphs 2 and 3, Bryson reveals his thoughts about certain aspects of Canberra. He does not state most of these directly, but we can work out or **infer** what he thinks.

For each of the following quotations, choose the answer that best sums up what we can infer (work out) about his opinions.

a) 'The Hotel Rex was exactly what you would expect a large hotel built of concrete and called the Rex to be.'

  i) He liked the hotel because it was large and strongly built and had a cute name that was easy to remember.

  ii) He didn't like the hotel much because it was unattractive in appearance and had a silly name more suited to a dog.

b) ' … you can water ski and shop for an evening gown and have a pizza all in the same day because this place has … *got it all!*'

  i) He felt the film showed that Canberra offered a weird assortment of things and boasted the place was much better than it really was.

  ii) He thought the film was informative and was impressed with the wide range of things that Canberra seemed to offer.

c) 'I watched the film happily because the room was air conditioned and it was a pleasure to sit after walking so far.'

  i) He enjoyed the film because the comfortable surroundings helped him concentrate and appreciate it.

  ii) He didn't think much of the film, but just took the opportunity for a rest in the comfortable, cool room as he was tired.

3 In paragraph 4 he describes getting lost on the way back to his hotel. Summarise the negative aspects of Canberra, which he reveals in this paragraph.

🔍 *Focus on style*

How does the writer put over his thoughts? Bill Bryson's style contains some noteworthy features:

1 It is very personal.

2 He uses hyperbole (exaggeration) for humorous effect.

3 It is chatty, addressing the reader directly.

4 He adopts a mocking tone through repetition.

5 He uses some very formal language in a deliberately pompous, tongue-in-cheek way, and combines this with very simple language.

◆ Select a **quotation** to illustrate each of these key features. (You will need **two quotations** for number 5.)

◆ Pick out any piece of writing from the extract that you find humorous and explain why you find it effective.

Word games

Choose a word from the box below that fits each of the following definitions.

● advertising or publicising

● skip playfully

● concerning Australia or New Zealand

● country/countryside (adjective)

● city (adjective)

● cheerful, optimistic

● changes, transforms

● broad avenue or main road

rural   morphs   urban   boulevard   upbeat   promotional   antipodean   gambol

☑ *Taking it further …*

New towns

Most towns and cities develop gradually and haphazardly over centuries. However, 'new towns' are specially planned settlements. Canberra was purpose-built in 1908 to be the seat of Australian government. Fifty years later, Brazil took the same approach with Brasilia, which was also specially founded as the capital of the country. Although these new cities have many good features they are sometimes criticised as being 'soulless' or even 'too tidy'.

In Scotland, Edinburgh has a 'new town' that was designed in the late eighteenth century as an improvement on the overcrowded 'old town' clustered around the Royal Mile. Today, this area is considered an architectural gem. In the 1940s, East Kilbride and Glenrothes were established as new towns, and in the 1960s, Irvine, Cumbernauld and Livingstone. These new towns have attracted both praise and criticism.

Edinburgh's New Town – today this area is considered to be an architectural gem

◆ Choose **one** new town to research, and write a short report of your findings.

Further reading

Bill Bryson is a highly entertaining writer of travel books. If you enjoyed this extract, you could try reading the rest of the book, which is very informative about Australia. Other books he has written include *Notes From a Big Country*, about his travels in the United States when he was a child, and *Notes From a Small Island* about his impressions of Great Britain when he arrived here as a young man. Any of his books would be suitable for a book report.

Inference

In interpreting the meaning of the passage on Canberra, you were asked to make 'inferences', that is, to work out what the writer was suggesting when he made certain comments. The writer was critical of some aspects of Canberra, but he made the criticisms **indirectly** by providing clues for the reader. For example, he did not say outright that he disliked the hotel, but hinted this by saying it was 'exactly what you would expect a large hotel built of concrete to be'. From this we deduced or **inferred** it was an ugly and unappealing building.

Inference means coming to a conclusion based on the facts and information that are given to you. We know that concrete is an ugly building material (compared with stone or marble, for example), and therefore a hotel built of concrete would probably be ugly. We can then **infer** that the writer found it ugly and did not like it.

An unappealing hotel building

✎ For practice

Look at these facts:

- Louise was expecting the postman to deliver a parcel when she was out at work.
- She had asked for it to be delivered to her neighbour instead.
- Her neighbour said she would phone when it arrived and Louise could collect it.
- When Louise came home she found a bank statement and an electricity bill in the letterbox.
- Her neighbour did not phone her.

From the facts, we can deduce or *infer* that:

- The postman had been to Louise's house that day.
- The parcel had not arrived.

Ancient Greek philosophers talked about *syllogisms:* statements that lead to a logical conclusion such as 'if A is true and B is true then C must be true'. A famous example of a syllogism goes as follows:

A All men are mortal.
B Greeks are men.
C Therefore all Greeks are mortal.

Of course, a syllogism has to be tested to see if it really makes logical sense.

A All cats have four legs.
B My dog has four legs.
C Therefore my dog is a cat.

The 1980s television comedy *Yes, Minister* came up with what has been dubbed 'the politician's syllogism'.

A To improve, things must change.
B We are changing things.
C Therefore, we are improving things.

Can you see the flaws in these examples? Try to find, or make up, some further examples of drawing the wrong inferences.

Be a detective

Inference skills would certainly be needed by anyone investigating a crime. Here is an extract from a recent novel, '*Bitter Water*' by Gordon Ferris, from the genre of crime fiction. It will provide an opportunity for you to develop your inferencing skills.

Friday morning found me gingerly picking my way over cobbles round the Gallowgate. The steaming piles of horse dung seemed as threatening as any minefield outside El Alamein. I was chasing the story about off-licence overpricing and the ensuing citizens' revolt. It was a patchy story, sparse on evidence but heavy on emotion. People take the price of drink seriously in that neck of the woods, especially on hot summer days. Some of the work-shy fancied a day out fishing in the Kelvin and had their minds set on chilling a couple of bottles in the river but the landlord's price hike had spoiled their wee picnic. A punch-up ensued. Windows got smashed. Heads got broken.

I thought I could squeeze a column out of it for the Monday edition to save me coming in on Sunday. In the absence of anything more thrilling before the closing bell I headed back to the news desk to type it up.

This time Morag brought the envelope to my desk. She looked so big-eyed and smiling that it would have been churlish of me not to invite her to the dancing on Saturday. I hoped I could remember how to Lindy Hop – if that's what they were still doing at the Locarno.

I turned over the missive. I felt a chill run through me. This was no *billet doux*. Same envelope, same handwriting as the first one. I opened it and read:

Dear Brodie,

I hope you're keeping count. Some have been found wanting and paid the penalty. Tell the others what to expect. Now you see how we deliver justice. No escape for the evil-doers!!! No legal tricks! We bring justice by the people to the people who deserve it.

The Glasgow Marshals

Same foaming rage as the first letter and with a clear warning of impending violence of a tougher, scarier order altogether.

Now you can infer

In the first two questions, choose the *most likely* option suggested; in the other questions, make your own suggestion of what can be inferred from the fact(s) given.

1   Reference is made to 'steaming piles of horse dung' and 'a minefield outside El Alamein' (a battle in the Second World War). We can therefore infer that:

 a) the story is about horses

 b) the story is set in the past, probably in the 1940s

 c) the story is about war

2   We are told that the narrator was 'chasing a story about off-licence overpricing' and he 'thought he could squeeze a column out of it for the Monday edition'. We can therefore infer that the writer's occupation is:

 a) a policeman

 b) a crime novelist

 c) a journalist

3   From the narrator's words: 'In the absence of anything more thrilling before the closing bell', we can infer that his opinion of the off-licence story is that …

4   From 'This time Morag brought the envelope to my desk', we can infer that …

5   From 'I hoped I could remember how to Lindy Hop – if that's what they were still doing at the Locarno (dance hall)', we can infer that …

6   From 'Some have been found wanting and paid the penalty. Tell the others what to expect', we can infer that …

◆   Now copy and complete the table below to review your progress.

Progress review	Yes
I can read a text with understanding.	
I can identify the purpose of a text.	
I can identify the main concerns of the text, and the supporting details and evidence that back them up.	
I can express my enjoyment and interest and give reasons, with evidence, for my personal response.	
I can make inferences from key statements.	
I can state these accurately in my own words.	

Chapter 2

Genre

The word 'genre' means type of writing. The term is used to describe wide categories, such as fiction or non-fiction, but it is also applied to smaller categories within these. It is useful to be able to identify the genre of a piece of writing as this will help you to recognise aspects of the writing that are characteristic of it.

In choosing to write in a particular genre, writers will have a particular readership in mind. For example:

- Some books on academic subjects are aimed at experts and assume specialist knowledge on the part of the reader, while others aim to make the topic accessible to the general reader. The former books will include technical language and jargon, while the latter will be written more simply and explain any obscure terminology used.

- Children's books may be fiction or non-fiction, but will be expressed in very simple language suited to the age group.

- Journalists who write for 'serious' newspapers such as *The Times*, the *Independent* or the *Guardian* use more complex language than those who write for the tabloids. 'Red top' papers such as the *Daily Record* or the *Sun* use short paragraphs and fairly simple language.

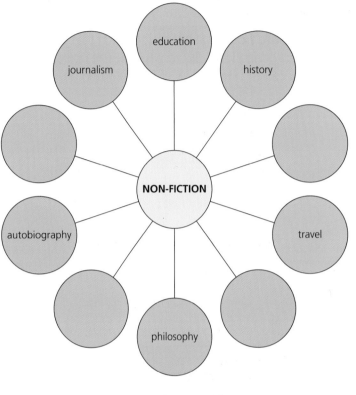

Non-fiction

There are many different non-fiction genres and in your external question paper there could be an extract from any one of them. The spider diagram shows some of the genres of non-fiction.

◆ Can you think of some more popular non-fiction topics to complete this spider diagram?

Fiction

The term '**general fiction**' is applied to novels that cannot be categorised in any particular way.

'**Literary fiction**' is the term used for novels that are of perceived literary merit, in terms of their subject matter, characterisation and style. Books in this genre are the ones that usually win major literary awards such as the Booker or Orange prizes.

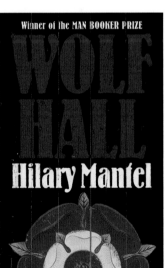

Literary fiction always has an important underlying **message** or **theme** that the writer intends to convey.

- It will explore some aspect of life or society.
- The characters will be fleshed out and interesting psychologically.
- It will aim to make the reader think more deeply about some aspect of the world.

'**Genre fiction**' is a term for fiction that is easily categorised into different types. The spider diagram shows a few of the common ones.

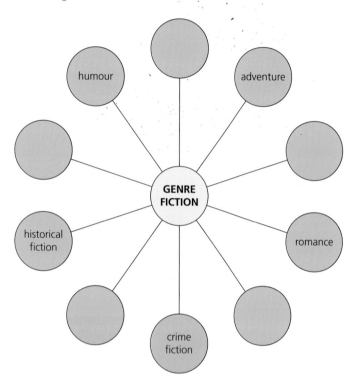

◆ Can you think of some other popular types of genre fiction to fill in this diagram?

Different fiction genres have their own '**conventions**', or elements that a reader expects to find. For example, in crime fiction, conventions include a murder plot, which is solved by a detective from a group of suspects. In the case of fantasy, readers expect to encounter strange, alternative worlds, characters with bizarre names and references to magic.

Purpose

In the case of most genre fiction, the main purpose is to entertain the reader. Themes are likely to be simple, such as good overcoming evil,

or evil being punished. Such fiction is often plot driven and characters may be stereotypes, for example appearing as typical heroes or villains.

For discussion

Brainstorm with a partner or small group the kind of characters you would associate with the following fiction genres:

- westerns
- science-fiction
- period drama
- spy thriller
- fantasy
- another genre of your own choice

Deciding on the genre

Personal or impersonal?

When you have to assign a piece of writing to a genre, think first whether it is written in the **first person** (using 'I', 'me', 'we') or the **third person** (using 'he', 'she', 'they'). Some genres, such as autobiography or diary, will always use first person, while others, such as history or biography, use the third person.

Sometimes the writer's personality and opinions come across strongly: this is known as a **personal** style. Where this does not happen, the style is said to be '**impersonal**'.

Novels may be written in either the first or the third person. A first person narrative may promote a stronger sense of realism, but limits the writer to one character's viewpoint.

> My father's family name being Pirrup, and my Christian name Philip, my infant tongue could make of both names nothing longer or more explicit than Pip. So, I called myself Pip, and came to be called Pip.
>
> I give Pirrip as my father's family name, on the authority of his tombstone and my sister – Mrs Joe Gargery who married the blacksmith.

◆ The extract is from the opening of Charles Dickens' novel, *Great Expectations*. What **person** has Dickens chosen? Is the style personal or impersonal?

The topics of **formal and informal** language and **dialect** are looked at in more detail in chapter 4 'The spoken word' (see pages 32–41).

Formal or informal?

A writer will choose the style that is most appropriate to the genre.

A **formal** style is used for academic topics and for some serious journalism. An **informal** style is preferred by a columnist giving a personal viewpoint. Novels written in the third person are likely to be more formal in style than those written in the first person. A first-person narrator will often give the impression of chatting with the reader, as if to a friend, using slang and conversational phrases. A famous example is the first few words of *The Catcher in the Rye*: 'If you really want to hear about it …'.

Look out for the use of **dialect** (the type of language used in a particular area, such as Glasgow). This produces a chatty, informal tone since dialect is largely used in spoken language. (You will find a good example of this in extract 12 on page 22.)

Presentation

Often the appearance of a page will give clues to the genre.

Specialist textbook

A specialist textbook (see below) will often use small print with italics, brackets and bold type for sub-sections. It may include diagrams, tables and graphs.

Children's books

Children's books will have large print, few words on each page and probably lots of colourful pictures.

Tabloid newspaper

In tabloid newspapers articles are broken up into short sections with sub-headings.

Simplifying algebraic fractions

Fractions can be simplified if the numerator and the denominator have a common factor.
In its **simplest form**, the numerator and denominator of an algebraic fraction have no common factor other than 1.

The numerator and denominator of $\frac{15}{25}$ have a highest common factor of 5.

$$\frac{15}{25} = \frac{15 \div 5}{25 \div 5} = \frac{3}{5}$$

3 and 5 have no common factors, other than 1.

$\frac{15}{25} = \frac{3}{5}$ in its simplest form.

Algebraic fractions work in a similar way.

> To write an algebraic fraction in its simplest form:
> - factorise the numerator and denominator of the fraction,
> - divide the numerator and denominator by their highest common factor.
>
> This is sometimes called **cancelling** a fraction.

Example 1

Write the following in their simplest form.

(a) $\dfrac{3x - 6}{3} = \dfrac{3(x - 2)}{3} = x - 2$

(b) $\dfrac{3x + 9}{4x^2 + 12x} = \dfrac{3(x + 3)}{4x(x + 3)} = \dfrac{3}{4x}$

(c) $\dfrac{x^2 y + 3xy^2}{xy - 2x^2 y^2} = \dfrac{xy(x + 3y)}{xy(1 - 2xy)} = \dfrac{x + 3y}{1 - 2xy}$

(d) $\dfrac{x^2 + 5x + 6}{x^2 - 2x - 8} = \dfrac{(x + 2)(x + 3)}{(x + 2)(x - 4)} = \dfrac{x + 3}{x - 4}$

(e) $\dfrac{x^2 + 2x + 1}{x^2 - 1} = \dfrac{(x + 1)^2}{(x + 1)(x - 1)} = \dfrac{x + 1}{x - 1}$

(f) $\dfrac{9 - 3y}{y - 3} = \dfrac{3(3 - y)}{y - 3} = \dfrac{-3(y - 3)}{y - 3} = -3$

A specialist textbook

A tabloid newspaper

For practice

Here is a list of different genres:

a) humorous novel
b) philosophy book aimed at the general reader
c) personal journal
d) psychology textbook
e) autobiography
f) news report
g) fantasy novel
h) history book aimed at the general reader
i) review in the Arts section of a newspaper
j) children's book
k) crime novel
l) article in the travel section of a newspaper

The extracts that follow are examples of each of these genres. There is **one** example of each of the genres in the list above (the sources are listed on page 97).

- First, read the extracts, and think about which genre each piece of writing belongs to.

- Copy down the letters a–l as a list in one column. Opposite, write down the number of the extract that you think is the example of that genre.

- **For each extract, copy and complete the checklist** below by ticking the relevant boxes. Discuss your answers with your class or group. Be prepared to justify your choice.

First person	Personal style	Formal language	Complex language and sentence structures	Dialogue; direct speech	Imagery (similes, metaphors)	Many adjectives; descriptive language	Fiction
Third person	Impersonal style	Informal language, slang	Simple language and sentences	No speech	No imagery	Little description	Non-fiction

Extract 1

A ball of ice from a jet crashed through the roof of a bungalow and shattered across an elderly couple's living room floor. It is thought to have fallen from an aeroplane thousands of feet above Paul and Deirdre Walker's home in Ashbourne, Derbyshire, yesterday. The frozen mass punched a hole through the roof and the plastered ceiling about a foot in diameter. It is thought that the lump was ice that built up on a wing or undercarriage and broke away as the landing gear came down. Mr Walker, 76, a retired aerospace chemist, and his 75-year-old wife, were about 10ft away from the point of impact when they heard a loud bang. The grandfather of three said: 'It sounded like someone had pushed over a glass cabinet, it was an enormous bang followed by a crashing noise.'

Extract 2

Seven people were assembled at Littlegreen House.

Hercule Poirot stood by the mantelpiece. Charles and Theresa were on the sofa, Charles on the arm of it with his hand on Theresa's shoulder. Dr Tanios sat in a grandfather chair. His eyes were red-rimmed and he wore a black band round his arm.

On an upright chair by a round table sat the owner of the house, Miss Lawson. She, too, had red eyes. Her hair was even untidier than usual. Dr Donaldson sat directly facing Poirot. His face was quite expressionless.

My interest quickened as I looked at each face in turn.

In the course of my association with Poirot I had assisted at many such a scene. A little company of people, all outwardly composed, with well-bred masks for faces. And I had seen Poirot strip the mask from one face and show it for what it was – *the face of a killer!*

Yes, there was no doubt of it. *One of these people was a murderer!* But which? Even now I was not sure.

Poirot cleared his throat – a little pompously as was his habit – and began to speak.

'I protest,' Miss Lawson tossed her head angrily. 'Disgraceful, that's what it is! Disgraceful!'

'Be patient, mademoiselle,' said Poirot. 'Be kind enough not to interrupt.'

Extract 3

Not everyone reacts to stress in the same way – and something that may cause a lot of stress to one person, may have little or no effect on another. Each person responds to a potentially stressful situation in a different way. It is not so much the situation itself, or the individual, but the interaction between the two that triggers the stress response. It is the judgement, or perception, that a person makes about the demands of the situation and their ability to cope with those demands.

Some people have an 'internal locus of control', whereby they feel they are responsible for what happens to them in their lives – whether good or bad. When things go well they feel good about themselves, if things go wrong they feel bad, but have the sense that they are in control of their own lives. These individuals generally cope better with stress as they feel they can influence what happens to them and take measures to counteract the influences of stress.

Other people have an 'external locus of control' and believe that things happen to them rather than them controlling their lives. If things go wrong then someone or something else is to blame. If things go right then it is just fate or good luck. These individuals do not cope so well with stress. They are very passive in their response, believing that whatever they do will have little effect, so they might just as well accept things as they are. This lack of perceived control can increase the levels of stress.

Extract 4

In Moulmein, in Lower Burma, I was hated by large numbers of people – the only time in my life that I have been important enough for this to happen to me. I was sub-divisional police officer of the town, and in an aimless, petty kind of way, anti-European feeling was very bitter. No one had the guts to raise a riot, but if a European woman went through the bazaars alone somebody would probably spit betel juice over her dress. As a police officer, I was an obvious target and was baited whenever it seemed safe to do so. In the end, the sneering faces of young men that met me everywhere, the insults hooted after me when I was at a safe distance, got badly on my nerves. The young Buddhist priests were the worst of all. There were several thousands of them in the town, and none of them seemed to have anything to do except stand on street corners and jeer at Europeans. All this was perplexing and upsetting. For at that time I had already made up my mind that imperialism was an evil thing and the sooner I chucked up my job and got out of it the better. Theoretically – and secretly, of course – I was all for the Burmese, and all against their oppressors, the British. As for the job I was doing, I hated it more bitterly than I can perhaps make clear.

Burma in 1935

Extract 5

Bourne himself, aka Matt Damon, didn't sign up to *The Bourne Legacy*, this fourth in the acclaimed espionage franchise. Instead, meet Aaron Cross (action star Jeremy Renner), a genetically enhanced super-agent in another, different, secret CIA programme. When a chilly agency bigwig (Ed Norton) decides to terminate both the programme and its agents, Cross goes on the global run, scooping up Rachel Weisz's blubbing scientist en route. A pay-attention story takes blooming ages to get off the blocks. Brace yourself for a whole lot of serious-faced exposition in dull rooms and not nearly enough pulse-pounding running about. The action, when it does come, is in frustrating fits and starts and never fully repays the wait – for example, there's a sub-*Tomorrow Never Dies* chase across shanty town rooftops. Like Jason Bourne, Aaron Cross is ever a cipher but Renner, an impressive actor (elsewhere), takes that the wrong way: beaming with all the charisma of a crossword puzzle. Still, he wrestles a good wolf. Aim expectations at kneecap level and this delivers a decent, over-talky, thriller. There's a reason why they called the last Bourne the 'Ultimatum'.

Extract 6

Once upon a time there was a poor miller who had three sons. When he died he left nothing but his mill, his donkey and his cat. The mill was left to his eldest son. The donkey was left to his second son. All that was left for the youngest son was the cat. He felt that was very unfair. 'My brothers can get together and make a living. What use is a cat? I shall starve,' complained the young man.

'Do not despair, master,' said the cat. 'If you will just give me a pair of boots and a bag, I promise you will find that we are not so badly off as you think.'

The miller's son was very surprised to find that the cat could talk. He was doubtful about what the cat had promised, but he thought to himself, 'A cat that can talk is special. I will do as he asks.' So with his last few coins he bought a pair of boots and a bag for the cat.

Extract 7

A 90-minute drive from Dalaman airport is the D-Hotel Maris, an example of Turkey's efforts to improve its tourism reputation and offer those who can afford it a higher standard of holiday. It's described as a 'design resort', a vast marble hotel that sprawls lazily around five biscuit-coloured beaches and inside has tasteful furnishings all carefully angled towards the sea, happy staff and the welcome whisper of high-end air conditioning. All of the 200 rooms look out on the protected bay below, with many of the balconies concealing bathtubs, from which guests can see, in the distance, the meeting point of the Aegean and the Mediterranean sea.

Upstairs on the executive floor, the presidential suite climbs over two levels with its own roof terrace and kitchen. Hire a villa and you get your own butler. This is no Butlins. Stress comes from choosing your beach. Do I want the long white beach by the restaurant that has a chilled 'dessert room'? Or the silent beach, where children are banned? In the three nights I spent here, tanning slowly in the lake-like sea, I relaxed to a dangerous degree. On day two at the breakfast buffet, I'd reached the point where I was garnishing my pancakes with kiwi. Garnishing! It feels perilously luxurious – worryingly wonderful. There are no stag weekends, no children throwing sand, or burger buffets. You will expect more from a Turkish break after a stay here.

Visit at your own risk.

Extract 8

'Lord King, I have just regained the fortress – and now you tell me I must leave again. I have the right to know your reason for such a command.' There was, perhaps, more outraged protest in Aldric's voice than proper courtesy permitted to be used towards the king, but Rynert let it pass. They were alone in the Great Hall and the king's footsteps were echoing in the emptiness as he paced to and fro.

'The oath made to your father commanded you to kill,' said Rynert. He paused in his incessant pacing and gazed at the wall, looking beyond it to the battlefield of Radmur Plain and the great pyres which still smouldered there. 'And you fulfilled your oath. Oh, yes. No man can deny it – least of all Kalarr.' His voice hardened. 'And Duergar. After the way you dealt with him …'

So that was it, thought Aldric grimly. Use of sorcery.

'Aldric Bladebearer Deathbringer,' muttered the king. 'You have something of a reputation already, my lord. A reputation for strangeness, too. You are … unusual. And you dismay people.'

'People?' Aldric wondered, as suspiciously as he dared.

'My other lords. The way in which you recovered this fortress and fulfilled the oath made to your father was unconventional. You have an aptitude for sorcery and no compunction about using it. Furthermore, you are a wizard's fosterling.'

Extract 9
14th May 1942

Two boys, perhaps twelve and six, come towards me on a narrow pavement. Tussling as they pass me, the older one catapults his brother at me and shouts out 'Jew!' It is ever more difficult to endure all this humiliation. And always the fear of the Gestapo.

15th May 1942

At Georgsplatz some packers from Thamm were working. One immediately came towards me, holding out his hand. 'It is very kind of you to shake my hand' (it is more than kind, it is a dangerous demonstration). 'How are you doing?' – 'Badly, very badly.' – 'Some time you'll have to tell me more about it.' He then went back to his van.

Both yesterday and today depressing because of the German victory at Kerch.

Frau Ida Kreidl, whom I met while I was shopping, reported the latest decree, she then showed it to us in the Jewish Community Newspaper: Jews with the star and anyone who lives with them are, with immediate effect, forbidden to keep pets (dogs, cats, birds), it is also forbidden to give the animals away to be looked after. This is the death sentence for our cat Muschel, whom we have had for more than eleven years.

18th May 1942

The Neumanns were here on Saturday. We heard bad news; the intention is evidently to wear us down, as many individuals as possible are to be driven to suicide. Dr Magnus, the orthopaedist with whom I shovelled snow, was stopped on Stübelplatz. A man jumped out of a Gestapo car: 'You wretch, why are you walking around here, why aren't you at work?' And spat in his face.

Extract 10

There were several changes in feeding habits among the Scots in the eighteenth century. Most of these factors would improve nutrition and raise resistance to disease. But exceeding them in importance, because more widespread geographically and socially, was the arrival of the potato as a common field crop. William Marshall called it 'the greatest blessing that modern times have bestowed on the country'. The significance of the potato was three-fold. Firstly, it helped to balance the national diet and to eliminate scurvy. Secondly, it provided for the first time an alternative staple to oatmeal that in previous centuries had supported the Scots through thick and thin; a peasant could now hope to raise more children if he could supplement the family's ordinary meal allowance with quantities of potatoes grown on his own rig or in his own yard. Thirdly, the potato could be used as a lifeline when there was a bad failure of the oat crop.

Extract 11

Although newspapers and magazines regularly show images of beautiful people, places and things, it is rare to come across an article that actually tries to explain what beauty is. And those few pieces are almost always devoted to a single theory: the theory of proportion. Typically they cite research carried out on the faces of film stars – Marilyn Monroe tends to be the first choice. It is then noted that the features of her face exhibit certain simple ratios. Her forehead is precisely as high as her nose is long; the space between her nostrils and her upper lip is one third the length of her nose; and so on. From this the conclusion seems to follow that beauty is a matter of proportion. This is not a new idea; it is, in fact, the oldest idea about the nature of beauty.

Extract 12

Ma Da's a nutter. Radio rental. He'd dae anything for a laugh so he wid; went doon the shops wi a perra knickers on his heid, tellt the wifie next door we'd won the lottery and were flittin tae Barbados, but that wis daft stuff compared tae whit he's went and done noo. He's turnt intae a Buddhist.

At first Ma thought it wis another wanny his jokes.

'Ah'm just gaun doon the Buddhist Centre for a couple hours, Liz, ah'll no be lang.'

'Aw aye, is there free bevvy there?'

'Naw, hen, ah'm serious. Just thought ah'd go and have a wee meditate, try it oot, know?'

Mammy turnt roond fae the washin up, and gied him wanny they looks, wanny they 'whit's he up tae noo?' looks ah'd seen a million times afore.

Taking it further

Which of the above extracts did you find most interesting?

Choose **one** extract. Make some more detailed notes on the ideas, language and style of the extract and then

EITHER:

Give a short talk to your class or group, explaining why it appealed to you. If your choice is one of the complete pieces, explain why you would like to read others of the same type. If it is one of those taken from a book, explain why you would like to read more of the book. You may also say which genre you would be *least* likely to seek out in your private reading, giving your reasons.

OR:

Write a report on your chosen extract, using quotations to illustrate the ideas, language and style that have impressed you.

Word games

First complete all the words below to give the genre of each of the different pieces of writing described and then find them in the wordsearch.

1 Genre with plot involving detection of murder and robberies: C _ _ _ _

2 Story of a person's life, written by the person: A _ _ _ _ _ _ _ _ _ _ _ _

3 Story of a person's life, written by someone else: B _ _ _ _ _ _ _ _

4 Story with the theme of love: R _ _ _ _ _ _

5 A story with a plot driven by suspense: T _ _ _ _ _ _ _

6 A book describing the writer's journeys: T _ _ _ _ _

7 Writing based on fact: N _ _ F _ _ _ _ _ _

8 Story set in the future or on another planet: S _ _ _ _ _ _ F _ _ _ _ _ _

9 Writing that discusses past events: H _ _ _ _ _ _

10 Writing found in newspapers and magazines: J _ _ _ _ _ _ _ _ _

11 Writing that is made up, not real: F _ _ _ _ _ _

12 A type or branch of writing: G _ _ _ _

13 A story set in a made-up world: F _ _ _ _ _ _

14 Writing giving an opinion on a book or film: R _ _ _ _ _

15 A children's story from folklore, based on magic: F _ _ _ _ _ _ _ _

K	J	V	M	X	U	E	F	N	P	Q	R	R	O	R
R	O	U	I	M	T	D	M	O	A	U	E	O	Y	J
B	U	E	L	A	T	Y	R	I	A	F	L	M	U	Y
M	R	G	N	N	Z	B	X	T	R	V	L	A	U	S
W	N	N	G	O	Z	G	N	C	B	C	I	N	W	W
N	A	C	H	Q	N	O	E	I	M	J	R	C	H	T
H	L	W	O	W	I	F	O	F	R	E	H	E	R	J
K	I	I	O	T	K	G	I	E	B	L	T	A	P	E
S	S	S	C	G	R	W	P	C	C	B	V	R	M	R
S	M	I	T	A	S	U	S	N	T	E	B	N	Z	N
M	F	V	P	O	K	E	Q	E	L	I	N	Y	T	E
S	F	H	M	P	R	W	X	I	F	J	O	Y	R	G
C	Y	D	R	Y	L	Y	B	C	F	R	L	N	Q	Y
I	F	A	N	T	A	S	Y	S	W	E	I	V	E	R
D	A	U	T	O	B	I	O	G	R	A	P	H	Y	Y

◆ Now copy and complete the table below to review your progress.

Progress review	Yes
I can identify the genre of a text.	
I can compare and contrast different types of text.	
I can identify similarities and differences between different types of text.	
I can explain why I prefer certain texts and authors.	
I can identify sources to develop the range of my reading.	

Chapter 3
Working with newspapers

One of the most effective ways of expanding your vocabulary and improving your written style of expression is to read quality journalism.

As many exam papers come from quality newspapers, reading such material is a good way of becoming familiar with the kind of passages you are likely to meet in the 'reading for understanding, analysis and evaluation' section of the exam.

At one time, newspapers used to be categorised as *tabloids* (small format papers with popular appeal) or *broadsheets* (large format papers with more in-depth articles). This distinction is no longer as clear cut as many broadsheets, such as *The Times*, have 'downsized' to a smaller format while retaining the same journalistic approach. Another change is that, with the development of the internet, most major newspapers now have websites where the day's articles can be read online, though some of these sites charge a subscription.

Some years ago an American journalist, Haydn Shaugnessy, wrote an influential piece entitled 'Ten things that will happen to TV and newspapers' in which he imagined what the fate of newspapers might be in the future. Here are some of his predictions:

- Newspapers will have a much reduced physical presence on newsstands and on shop counters as they deploy their online strategies and will realise belatedly that physical distribution gave them the kind of presence only the milkman and the baker dreamed of. The result will be a much reduced influence in their new online role.

- As all information will be free to the end-user, everybody in news production will have to go to the advertiser-pool for every cent that it takes. News bureaux around the world will close and the authoritative 'source' will become the local blogger-pool.

- What you know will become more a case of what can you believe and who else believes it too. Confusion and uncertainty will have an impact on social and political life.

It is certainly true that we no longer need to rely on the morning paper to find out what is happening locally or in the world, as such information can be picked up more quickly from radio, television or from the 'breaking news' that is constantly available online.

However, newspapers do not only report news: they can reflect, comment on and analyse what is happening. This is usually done in *feature articles,* which provide discussion and analysis of issues in the news, and in *editorials* in which the newspaper gives its own opinion on an event – these may be influenced by some form of bias as when, for example, a newspaper tends to support one political party against the others.

Besides bias, other **criticisms of newspapers** are that they can:

- be intrusive into people's privacy
- report inaccurately or sensationalise events in order to sell more copies
- influence, or distort, people's thinking by treating minor events as major ones and vice versa. As the Irish playwright George

Bernard Shaw once put it, '… newspapers are unable seemingly to discriminate between a bicycle accident and the collapse of civilization'.

What do you think?

♦ Do some research on one of the following issues. Your findings could then be discussed in a group or presented to the class as an individual talk.

- Will the online news replace newspapers?
- Is it important that newspapers have the freedom to investigate and publish stories that the people involved might want to cover up?
- Does the press intrude into people's lives (particularly celebrities)?
- Do newspapers influence people's thinking? Is this a good or a bad thing?

The rest of this chapter looks at some newspaper articles and provides practice in **understanding ideas, analysing style** and **evaluating arguments**.

Two newspaper articles on the need for speed

The following two articles were written in response to the news that the government was considering increasing the speed limit on motorways from 70 mph to 80 mph. One writer was against this change and the other was in favour.

No!

1 I have a confession. To my shame I have been known to break the speed limit. I suspect I am not alone. Indeed, on some motorways, motorists driving at 70 mph are the ones pootling in the slow lane. While not exactly Mr Toad, I am not one of life's pootlers.

2 So at first sight, the proposals from the Transport Secretary do appear attractive. They have the virtue of recognising the reality of what is happening on our motorways. Of course, cars are safer and handle better than they did when the 70 mph limit was set. It is probably a vote-winner as well.

3 In short, raising the limit seems such a no-brainer, one has to ask why was it not done before.

4 Alas there are rather good reasons for doing nothing and leaving well alone. Similar proposals were kicked around the Department for Transport while the last government was in power. The idea was that the limit would be increased to 80 mph and – this is the key part – strictly enforced.

5 Without strict enforcement, the *de facto*¹ limit would have risen to 90 mph. This is because of guidelines drawn up by the Association of Chief Police Officers, which allow a margin for error of 10 per cent plus 2 mph. This margin is needed to take into account faulty car speedometers and, perish the thought, the possibility that speed cameras might not be totally accurate.

6 The previous government was not altogether comfortable with the idea of cars hurtling along at 90 mph. Given the problems of enforcement, it quietly ditched the proposals.

7 But, unless the government is comfortable with raising the *de facto* – as opposed to *de jure*² – speed limit to 90 mph, similar questions still remain.

8 How will the new limit be enforced? One option is the installation of speed cameras across the entire motorway network. But the cameras would cost a vast amount of money which, given the state of public finances, may not be particularly easy to find.

9 The alternative is to follow the French example. There, the speed limit is higher, but motorists run the gauntlet of the rather terrifying traffic police. Judging by the French television broadcasts I have seen, the police track motorists from the air, with speed guns and the kind of hi-tech equipment which one associates with RoboCop.

10 There are many arguments in favour of pushing the legal maximum up to 80 mph. It is a limit that would go with rather than against the grain of current motoring behaviour.

11 But the practicalities of making the policy work will need to be thought out and the conclusion may be that the messy compromise we have at the moment, with police enforcing 70 mph with a sensitive and light touch, has a lot to recommend it.

David Millward

¹*de facto: in fact, whether allowed by law or not*
²*de jure: by law*

⊕ *Taking a closer look*

🔎 *Focus on meaning*

1 This article begins in a personal way. What is the writer's 'confession'?

2 Given that he is against raising the speed limit, what advantage do you think he gains by beginning in this way?

3 What are the three reasons in favour of raising the speed limit that the writer gives in paragraph 2?

4 Explain in your own words the distinction he is making between *de facto* and *de jure* speed limits (paragraphs 5 and 7).

5 What does the writer consider to be the main problem with the proposal to increase the speed limit?

6 How is this matter dealt with in France (paragraph 9)?

7 **In your own words**, explain the 'messy compromise' that currently exists (paragraph 11).

8 Which of the following statements are true and which are false?

a) The writer thinks that, at first sight, raising the speed limit sounds like a good idea.

b) The previous government considered raising the speed limit on motorways to 90 mph.

c) If the law was changed to raise the speed limit to 80 mph, the *de facto* speed limit would be nearer 90 mph.

d) If the law was changed to raise the speed limit to 80 mph, the *de jure* speed limit would be nearer 90 mph.

e) The writer is opposed to an 80 mph speed limit in principle.

f) The writer does not object to an 80 mph speed limit in principle but believes it is not practical to have such a limit.

🔧 *Tools of the trade: topic sentences*

Like most passages of a factual or discursive nature, this one often uses a **topic sentence** at the start of a paragraph to indicate what the rest of the paragraph will deal with. Look at paragraph 2, for example:

> So at first sight, the proposals from the Transport Secretary do appear attractive. They have the virtue of recognising the reality of what is happening on our motorways. Of course, cars are safer and handle better than they did when the 70 mph limit was set. It is probably a vote-winner as well.

The first sentence is a topic sentence, stating that the proposals appear attractive. The remainder of the paragraph expands upon this by giving three reasons why a higher speed limit would make sense.

◆ Below are some other sentences from the article. Decide whether they are topic sentences or not.

1 'Alas there are rather good reasons for doing nothing and leaving well alone.'
2 'I suspect I am not alone.'
3 'How will the new limit be enforced?'
4 'Given the problems of enforcement, it quietly ditched the proposals.'
5 'The alternative is to follow the French example.'
6 'There are many arguments in favour of pushing the legal maximum up to 80 mph.'
7 'Judging by the French television broadcasts I have seen, the police track motorists from the air, with speed guns and the kind of hi-tech equipment which one associates with RoboCop.'

◆ Now look back at the ones you thought were topic sentences. What should they all have in common?

Yes!

1 More than 40 years after the 70 mph motorway speed limit was introduced, we have a Transport Secretary prepared to address the reality of life on our roads and suggest the possibility of raising the maximum to 80 mph, in the process banishing an anachronistic piece of Sixties' legislation.

2 Why all the fuss and furore? A 70 mph limit might have made sense in the mid-Sixties, when few cars were capable of travelling at sustained high speed, but most modern cars – even the venerable Land Rover Defender, which is among the slowest cars on sale today, can muster 82 mph – will easily cruise at 70 mph and more.

3 It's not just the engine technology that has advanced in leaps and bounds, but suspension, tyres and, crucially, braking systems. According to The Highway Code, the recommended stopping distance from 70 mph, including reaction time, is 96 metres or 315 feet. An average Volkswagen Golf, the biggest-selling car in Europe, is capable of stopping from the same speed in only 49.3 metres.

4 The suggestion to look at raising the limit to 80 mph certainly looks like a populist move. Indeed, a survey carried out for *Autocar* magazine this week reveals that 94.6 per cent of drivers admit to breaking the limit, including my esteemed colleague Mr Millward. If this is so, what's wrong with raising the maximum? Especially when the same survey shows that 6.1 per cent of respondents always break the motorway speed limit by 20 mph. Raising the limit wouldn't be *carte blanche* for drivers to set their own arbitrary limits.

5 And the move has been backed by the AA, although the motoring organisation proposes variable limits of up to 80 mph rather than a blanket maximum.

6 Of course there are downsides. Raising motorway speed limits to boost the economy? The only thing it will boost is fuel company profits, because no matter how frugal cars are these days it remains true that the faster you go the more fuel you use.

7   Road safety is the major sticking point, but it must be repeated that speed *per se* doesn't kill. It's a matter of appropriate speed. No one in their right mind would argue against driving at much reduced speed in adverse weather, particularly in the fog that afflicts many roads at this time of year. In good conditions, with a clear road, would it really be so outrageous to have a maximum of 100 mph? This system is at its best on French autoroutes. The 130 kph (81 mph) limit for good conditions works well. Crucially, French drivers observe the lower 110 kph (68 mph) limit in inclement weather.

8   The best part about the proposal is that it has reignited the debate about personal mobility and responsibility. We're a generally law-abiding lot so there won't be many tears shed if the whole thing gets quietly forgotten, as is likely – until the next time a Transport Secretary dares to raise the question.

Paul Hudson

🔍 Focus on structure

In argumentative writing of this kind, it is best not to pack too many points into one paragraph as this can make the argument difficult to follow. This writer unfolds his argument in a step-by-step fashion, with each paragraph dealing with one main point.

Complete the sentences on each paragraph below by simply stating the main point of each paragraph. In other words, try to summarise the argument of the passage, missing out the examples and evidence. Paragraph 2 has been done for you.

In paragraph 1 the writer states his view that …

In paragraph 2 he explains that modern cars are capable of higher speeds.

In paragraph 3 …

In paragraphs 4 and 5 …

In paragraph 6 …

In paragraph 7 …

In paragraph 8 he draws his argument to a conclusion by …

Once you have summarised the passage, you will see that it is organised clearly as follows:

- **Paragraph 1**   Introduction
- **Paragraphs 2–5**   Reasons for raising the speed limit
- **Paragraphs 6–7**   Reasons against raising the speed limit
- **Paragraph 8**   Conclusion

🔧 Tools of the trade: methods of persuasion

The writer uses a number of different techniques to take his readers along with him and convince us to share his opinion.

Statements and evidence

In writing of this kind it is not enough simply to make statements; they must be backed up with evidence. The evidence can take various forms:

- reference to a specific case or example
- statistical evidence
- quotations from those involved, such as experts

Sometimes the evidence will be introduced by an expression such as 'for example' or 'for instance'.

Look at paragraph 3.

It's not just the engine technology that has advanced in leaps and bounds, but suspension, tyres and, crucially, braking systems. According to The Highway Code, the recommended stopping distance from 70 mph, including reaction time, is 96 metres or 315 feet. An average Volkswagen Golf, the biggest-selling car in Europe, is capable of stopping from the same speed in only 49.3 metres.

The first sentence makes a **statement**: modern cars have improved in numerous ways, particularly regarding the brakes.

The second and third sentences expand on this by giving an **example** of how modern vehicles can stop in much shorter distances than those recommended in the Highway Code.

◆ From anywhere else in the passage, write down **two** examples of a statement and **two** examples of material used as back-up evidence.

Rhetorical questions

Another technique used to make an argument more convincing is the **rhetorical question**. This is a question that does not require an answer, either because the writer goes on to provide the answer, or because the writer is asking the reader to consider his or her own answers. The writer does this at the start of paragraph 2: 'Why all the fuss and furore?'

◆ From anywhere else in the passage, find another example of a rhetorical question.

Grasping the main points

You have now read two passages on the issue of an 80 mph motorway speed limit and will be aware of the main arguments on both sides.

Look back over the passages and write down the main points under the headings 'No: stick to 70' and 'Yes: change to 80' missing out the detailed evidence or the writers' personal feelings.

◆ Write a single paragraph of about 125 words, presenting both sides in a neutral, non-biased way. Remember to:

  ◆ Use linking words and phrases to make your paragraph flow.

  ◆ Write in a formal style – avoid abbreviations such as 'don't' (say 'do not') and any conversational or slang words (such as 'pootling' and 'no-brainer').

  ◆ Present the arguments in order of importance rather than as a simple list.

  ◆ Lead up to a concluding sentence where you say something like: '*Although there are many convincing arguments for/ against raising the speed limit, it would be more beneficial if [state your own position] because [give the main reason].*'

See chapter 5 on Body language for further practice in summarising skills.

Taking it further

◆ Find an article of your own, summarise it and identify features of style (topic sentences etc.) that you have been studying in this chapter.

◆ Suitable publications to use for this would be the *Scotsman*, the *Herald*, *The Times*, the *Guardian*, the *Independent* and the *Daily Telegraph*.

What do you think?

This debate led to readers posting numerous responses. Below is a selection of some of their comments.

● On reflection, and having previously been against it, I am now ambivalent towards it.

  The ones who think it will allow them to drive faster will attempt to do just that, whilst those LGVs restricted to 60 mph and those of us who prefer to save fuel and take our time can still pootle along at 65.

  The former will still have to avoid the latter, and nothing will ever change that.

● In these days of austerity and economic recession, the legal limit should be 60 mph. Speed burns fuel, costs money and fills the treasury coffers with the extra taxes. That's the real reason for the government wanting to lift the limit. People pay more tax by burning more fuel.

  How come there's never any congestion on a road with 50 mph average speed limit cameras?

● The debate isn't even worth having. Motorway traffic tends to run at 70–80 mph and the police have a well-known 10% error allowance on the 70 mph limit. Motorists believe they won't be prosecuted up to the 77 (80) mark.

What would be entirely logical and sensible would be to make the limit 80 and do away with the 10% tolerance. Police it properly at 80 – modern vehicles have very accurate odometers. Then everyone will know where they stand.

The current situation with the 70 limit being ignored by the majority of motorway users and by the police is farcical.

- We have a terrible standard of driving, more and more unlicensed, uninsured drivers, a poor method of testing and they want to INCREASE the limit?

Make the punishments for dangerous driving and driving uninsured fit the crimes with long prison sentences, stop ambulance chasers from staging accidents for profit and maybe, just maybe reconsider this in 10 years.

- 90 is a perfectly reasonable speed on a non-crowded motorway in good conditions. Anyone who's driven in Germany knows that 100 is a comfortable cruising speed for today's cars.

- Driving is a privilege not a right. The judicious use of speed has probably prevented more accidents than it has caused. Almost every driver will be able to recount stories of near misses with drunks and lunatics only avoided by putting the foot down. It seems almost inevitable that an increase to 80 will be accompanied by some such evil foolishness as 'strict enforcement', as a sop to the safety numpties and envirofascists. It will, at a stroke, eliminate most of the benefits of the change and, if anything, *increase* the burden of bureaucracy from speed tax enforcement.

Given the nature of government, this is exactly what will happen unless it is scotched early.

- Don't compare us to the French! They slaughter three times as many people on the roads as we do – tragically mostly younger drivers. What WE need is a minimum speed limit of 70 mph in the slow lane, 80 in the middle lane and 90 in the fast lane. Any driver trapped doing less than this would be banned automatically for 6 months – freeing up valuable road space and allowing people to reach their destinations more quickly.

◆ These responses illustrate many different language techniques. Choose any **three** of the above, and write a brief commentary on any of the language features the writer uses to convey his or her view. You may comment on the similarities or differences between the way writers express themselves.

Among the aspects of language you might consider are:

- ◆ sentence structure
- ◆ word choice
- ◆ emotive language
- ◆ rhetorical questions
- ◆ bias
- ◆ logical (or illogical) argument
- ◆ use of evidence
- ◆ tone (such as humorous or ironic tone)
- ◆ any other feature.

◆ Imagine you have decided to post your own response to the articles or to any of the views above. Write your opinion, using an appropriate style of expression, in no more than 100 words.

Word games

Match up the words in the box with a suitable definition. The first two definitions come from the 'NO' article and the rest from the 'YES' article.

1 Settling an argument by finding a middle way between two opinions: _ _ _ _ _ _ _ _ _ _

2 Ensuring that a law is obeyed: _ _ _ _ _ _ _ _ _ _ _

3 Out of date, belonging to another period of time: _ _ _ _ _ _ _ _ _ _ _ _ _

4 Rage, uproar, fury: _ _ _ _ _ _

5 By or in itself (Latin): _ _ _ / _ _

6 Highly valued: _ _ _ _ _ _ _ _

7 Giving someone freedom to act as they wish (French): _ _ _ _ _ / _ _ _ _ _ _ _

8 A choice or decision made entirely on the basis of personal opinion or random factors, rather than on valid reasons: _ _ _ _ _ _ _ _ _

9 Economical, sparing: _ _ _ _ _ _

10 Severe (of weather): _ _ _ _ _ _ _ _ _

11 Ability to move around: _ _ _ _ _ _ _ _

frugal	esteemed	inclement	venerable	per se	anachronistic	mobility
enforcement		carte blanche	arbitrary		compromise	furore

If you have matched up the words and definitions correctly, you will be left with one word which means 'entitled to respect as a result of being around for a long time'.

◆ Now copy and complete the table below to review your progress.

Progress review	Yes
I can identify the main ideas in a passage.	
I can present these in the form of a summary in a single paragraph.	
I can distinguish between statements and evidence.	
I can identify techniques used to persuade the reader such as rhetorical questions and emotive language.	

Chapter 4
The spoken word

In this chapter we will examine some of the ways in which spoken language differs from written language by looking at two pieces of text.

1 For your ears only: an interview with Daniel Craig

The first piece of text is a transcript of an interview – a written form of the exact words spoken when Dave Calhoun of *Time Out London* met current 007 actor Daniel Craig and put some questions to him that he had gathered from a few acquaintances who had either been involved with or connected to James Bond.

David Calhoun: This first question is from Richard Kiel, who played Jaws in *The Spy Who Loved Me* and *Moonraker*. He wants to know: how has being Bond
5 changed your career? Have you been offered better roles because of it?

Daniel Craig: Yes, there's no doubt it's changed things. It might have been different if we hadn't had the success
10 we did with *Casino Royale*. It could have been more, let's say … interesting.

I may not have been offered all the jobs that you'd expect, but I've definitely been shown stuff I wasn't before. And it's
15 made me get more active about it. That's what I've always done, gone looking for scripts, and this has given me that extra push. I made *Defiance*, a World War II film, last year which was one of those roles that just got plumly offered to me. I don't think
20 that would have happened before.

David Calhoun: Who's your favourite male actor and have you tried to emulate him in any way?

Daniel Craig: The answer's no. Definitely not. I had a ton of people I admired (when I was starting out) but I was as fickle as I could possibly be. It depended on the movie I'd just seen. Literally. If I came running out of a movie, I was that person for at least 10 or 15 minutes. I was as fickle
25 as that. I didn't care as long as they were cool and good in that movie. I admire people like Paul Newman, the great modern movie actors such as Robert Redford and Steve McQueen. Those guys were not only great actors but movie stars as well.

David Calhoun: This question is from Dame Stella Rimington, former head of MI6. Have you ever met a real British intelligence officer and is your portrayal of Bond influenced in any way by that?

30 **Daniel Craig:**   Firstly, how would I know if I met a spy? Although I have met quite a few special forces guys who do a lot of covert work. On the whole, they're easier to recognise as they look like they can kill. They give off an aura of violence.

David Calhoun: So no spy has ever approached you in solidarity?

Daniel Craig: What? A nod and wink at me in a strange way? No. I'm not sure that's the answer
35 she's looking for.

David Calhoun: On the back of that, how have you found the public interest that comes with playing Bond? You must have had to consider that when you took the plunge?

Daniel Craig: Definitely. That was one of the many conversations I had with myself. When it came down to it, I decided to embrace the whole thing. There's no point doing a Bond movie – or a $200
40 million movie – and hiding away for 6 months. You have to get out there and do it, instead of thinking: 'I don't know if I can deal with this'. But on the whole I'm doing the same thing I've always done and trying to keep as private as I possibly can. Certainly, I've tried to keep my family and friends far away from it and I feel their privacy is crucially important.

David Calhoun: This is from John Cleese: How tall do you think Bond should be?

45 **Daniel Craig:**   Shorter than John Cleese! He's about 6'5'', I think.

David Calhoun: And one from Ann Carter, the head of exhibitions at the Imperial War Museum which has an Ian Fleming show on at the moment: How far have you based your Bond on your on-screen predecessors?

Daniel Craig: Not at all, really. Not deliberately.
50 I sat and watched every movie religiously. And I still do, I have them all in the trailer. I've become a nerd, basically. I feel I need to, it's part of what it is. But that was never the point. I could never start repeating it. I had to take it somewhere new. That said, I may start
55 doing Sean Connery impressions in the next one, just for the hell of it.

David Calhoun: Here's one from Charlie Higson, author of the 'Young Bond' books: How much of Fleming's Bond is there in Craig's Bond?

60 **Daniel Craig:**   I hope a lot, but it's subliminal. It's about reading the books. What I wanted to do with *Quantum of Solace* was to draw on Fleming's obsession with detail. He has two pages to describe making scrambled egg. Marc [Marc Forster, the film director]
65 wanted to turn that into cinematic detail, so that just looking at the frame is sumptuous.

Also, there's a darkness in the book *Casino Royale*, there's a fight in there. Here's a man (Bond) who's incredibly reluctant to do what he does, which I think applied
70 to Fleming too. He'd always have preferred to be at Goldeneye [his Jamaican villa] writing and taking gin fizzes at 11 o'clock in the morning. Wouldn't we all?

Tall man John Cleese

David Calhoun: I spoke to Marc Forster recently and he kept stressing the importance of character in this new film. Was that key?

75 **Daniel Craig:** I think so. Marc's Swiss – I mean this in the best way – he's very fastidious, very organised, which are qualities that lend themselves to a Bond movie. There's an efficiency that you need. I think my Bond is quite efficient, but ragged, if that makes sense. He efficiently kills people but everything blows up around him. I can't sing Marc's praises highly enough, he's a good man.

David Calhoun: Here's Sir Roger Moore. He wants to know: Who is your favourite Bond
80 between Sean Connery and Timothy Dalton?

Daniel Craig: [*Roars with laughter.*] It's you, Sir Roger! I'm a Connery fan, and he knows that. I've told lots of people. But I've got a big soft spot for Moore: *Live and Let Die* was the first movie I saw in the cinema with my dad. It was ridiculously camp – and then it just got camper.

David Calhoun: Sir Roger would also like to know if you'll be buying his new autobiography?

85 **Daniel Craig:** Probably. Can he not sign me a copy? I'll buy it. You made these questions up! You could have made these questions up…

David Calhoun: Are you enjoying these questions?

Daniel Craig: It's great, believe me it couldn't be a better way to start the day. They've been good questions.

90 **David Calhoun:** The Bond films are huge studio enterprises, but then there's the family element: the Flemings and the books, the Broccolis and the film legacy. How does that play out for you?

Daniel Craig: I don't think Michael or Barbara [respectively stepson and daughter of original Bond producer Cubby Broccoli] would mind me saying that the films are as close as you'll get to making a Hollywood movie away from home, but the way it's run is unique. It's all because of
95 them. It has total autonomy and their love of the product – the books – comes from Cubby and they guard it jealously. The Flemings are richer people because of the Broccolis, let's put it that way. It's a two-way street.

David Calhoun: Twenty-two films on, it's got to be hard to preserve that sense of wonder?

Daniel Craig: It is, but that's why Marc was so clever finding that Panama location. It's a place
100 called Colon, which is seriously depressed economically but wonderful. It's one of those magical places. And that's there on the screen. We also went to Chile. Marc pushed for that, he was so insistent on making the locations characters in this movie. Anything to keep it away from me, fine.

⊕ *Taking a closer look (speaking and writing)*

◆ How can you tell that this is a transcript of spoken words, rather than a piece of writing? Discuss this in your group, with the group leader collating a list of all the language features that mark this out as an example of oral communication.

You may have identified some of the following features. Copy and complete the table below by finding an example of each from anywhere in the extract.

Language feature	Example
Looser sentence structures (i.e. incomplete 'sentences' that do not follow the usual pattern of subject, verb etc.)	
Mixture of different registers (formal/informal)	
Use of rhetorical questions	
Expression of personal opinion	
Reference to personal experience (anecdote)	
Interaction between interviewer and interviewee (repartee)	

Tools of the trade: formal and informal register

This interview transcript should help you understand some of the following critical terminology.

Informal language

In everyday spoken communication we use:

- abbreviations (shortened forms of words) such as 'don't', 'can't', 'isn't'
- looser sentence structures (i.e. 'sentences' that are not full sentences, or which lack components such as the verb or subject)
- personal pronouns (I and you).

Formal language

In formal language, which is more likely to be used for written communication:

- Shortened forms are written out in full (do not, cannot, is not).
- Word choice is more precise, correct and perhaps more complicated.
- The tone will not be chatty or personal.
- There may be more emphasis on facts, information and ideas rather than on personal opinion and feelings.

Slang and jargon

Slang is an aspect of informal language involving non-standard word choice. An example from the interview would be 'I had a ton of people I admired'.

Jargon is an aspect of formal language in which words are used that have a special meaning connected with a particular area of study, profession etc. An example from the interview would be 'frame' (line 66), a term used in connection with films.

In real life, of course, language cannot be rigidly divided into 'formal' and 'informal'; as can be seen from the interview, a more formal style of expression is often used when a more serious or thoughtful point is being made.

For practice

Decide whether each of the following is formal or informal.

1 '... I've definitely been shown stuff I wasn't before.'
2 '... I have met quite a few special forces guys ...'
3 'Marc wanted to turn that into cinematic detail ...'
4 '... he was so insistent on making the locations characters in this movie.'
5 'I didn't care as long as they were cool ...'
6 'A place ... which is seriously depressed economically.'

Taking a closer look

Write down your answers to the questions below.

1 As you will probably have noticed, the tone of the interview varies considerably. At times it is light-hearted; at other times it is more serious and reflective; occasionally Craig is being careful and guarded so that he does not

offend significant people in the film industry.
Find examples of each of the following:

a) a light-hearted, humorous tone

b) a more serious and reflective tone

c) a careful and balanced standpoint

d) a strong statement of personal opinion or feeling

e) an answer that shows less certainty

2 What does Daniel Craig mean when he gives the following answers?

a) 'I decided to embrace the whole thing.' (line 39)

b) 'I've become a nerd, basically.' (lines 51–52)

c) 'I hope a lot, but it's subliminal.' (line 60)

d) 'There's a darkness in the book *Casino Royale* …'. (line 67)

e) 'I think my Bond is quite efficient, but ragged, if that makes sense.' (line 77)

Summarising the main points

In the following questions, you should summarise the main point Daniel Craig is making. Some line references are given to help you. Your answer should be in the third person rather than the first person, and you should write in a clear, factual style rather than trying to convey the speaker's feelings.

Example

Summarise Daniel Craig's answer to the first question 'how has being Bond changed your career?' (lines 4–5).

Answer

Daniel Craig's success in his first Bond film, *Casino Royale*, changed his career as it opened the door to other film opportunities. For example, he was offered a role in a film about the Second World War, which would not have happened before.

Now summarise the following points in the same way.

1 How does Daniel Craig see himself in relation to earlier actors who have played James Bond? (Use material from lines 49–56.)

2 What does Craig have to say about the relationship between the Bond films and the original James Bond books by Ian Fleming? (Use material from lines 60–66.)

3 What qualities does he think Marc Forster, the director, has? (Use material from lines 64–66 and lines 75–78.)

Word games

Match up the words in the box with a suitable definition.

I a feeling or atmosphere that can be detected from a person or place

2 changeable, unreliable in feelings

3 personal freedom and independence

4 careful, fussy, hard to please

5 undercover, secret

6 where filming takes place

7 lavish, luxurious

8 sticking together; supporting each other because both parties are in a similar situation

fastidious   covert   sumptuous   fickle   autonomy   subliminal   solidarity   aura   location

If you have matched up words and definitions correctly, you will be left with one word which means 'beneath the surface; not able to be seen or detected by other senses'.

For class discussion

'Press conference'

Each person in the class writes a question to be directed to a celebrity or famous person from history. The class agrees on one of these celebrities or famous people and four students are then selected to role play this person.

The rest of the class take it in turn to ask their questions. A scribe should also be appointed to transcribe (or even record) the interviews.

The questions and answers should then be transcribed *verbatim* (word for word). The transcript of the completed interview could then be used as a basis for group/class discussion in which aspects of language studied in this chapter can be identified.

2   Neighbourliness and the open door: life in Glasgow tenements in the 1940s

The second piece of writing we are looking at in this chapter is an extract from *Up Oor Close: Memories of Domestic Life in Glasgow Tenements, 1901–1945* by Jean Faley, Professor of Sociology in the University of Wisconsin, USA. She returned to Glasgow in the 1980s and interviewed old people about their memories.

'Up oor close': the phrase epitomises the sense of belonging, the sociability and the neighbourliness so keenly missed by people who remember the old tenements and the old times. The families sharing a close, or common entry way – leading to the back-close (the passage out to the shared back court) and the stairs to the houses on the upper floors – formed a mini-community.

… The close was the centre of life, and families were bonded by a friendliness which was a necessary lubricant of crowded living conditions … One or two women are remembered as the kind who were proprietorial about their back courts and would chase away children from another close. But these were the exceptions. The tenement house door in these days often stood open. This is recalled as another stark difference from today, with several eloquent testimonies to the general kindness and honesty of neighbours.

Ye could leave yer doors opened. I've seen every door being left opened on the landing. Every door, for three stairs up, every door left open. Oh, nae fear of burglars or anything like that.   (John Dowie)

There was a great homely feeling. If you lived in that block of red sandstone tenements across there, you never locked your door. I'm not saying that neighbours trailed in and out your house all day. But ye never locked your door. And if ye had children, they didnae play oot in the street. They played in the back court. And they came up and the door would be open, ye know, it would just be open. It would never be locked. (Mary Preece)

The open door was a manifestation of the neighbourly helpfulness and generosity which was indeed essential to survival – which provided a jug of soup for a family hit by unemployment, or parcelled out 'close' children to be cared for while a mother was in hospital.

I mean you always found somebody to help you. That was one thing about the place. There was always somebody to help you. Because your neighbours used to come in, and you could leave your door open. It's just a wee daft check key. And your neighbours could go in. If they wanted a wee bit butter they came in an' took a wee bit butter, an' if you needed sugar they gave you sugar. It was fantastic! It was more like the one big, big family. There was no quarrels. There was no bitterness.

There was very few house-breakings going on. People were in the same situation, nobody had anything worth stealing. Just family things. Although maybe the ornaments, they could have been pawned to get money. But nobody thought of sneaking in the way they do today. At that time, too, if anybody attacked an old person or a kid, the gangs at the street, to a boy, the big chaps, you know the corner fellows, got a hold of them. They'd give them a good hammering, you know. So old people could walk the streets without being mugged or anything. Safe. But the tough men, although they fought among themselves, respected age. (James Baxter)

⊕ Taking a closer look

The questions that follow will help you think about the writer's purpose, the use of statements and evidence, and the differences between **formal** and **informal** register.

What do you think the writer's main purpose is in this extract?

a) To show how living in tenements created a sense of community.

b) To draw attention to the problems of poverty and unemployment.

c) To show that crimes such as burglary and mugging were less common in the first half of the twentieth century.

As in much non-fiction writing, this extract combines **statements** and **evidence**. In the more formal passages the writer, a sociology professor in the USA, draws general conclusions; in the informal, spoken passages older people's memories are given as evidence of these general points.

What is the most suitable general conclusion that can be drawn from each of the following pieces of evidence?

1 *'If [your neighbour] wanted a wee bit butter they came in an' took a wee bit butter, an' if you needed sugar they gave you sugar.'*

a) Foods like butter and sugar were in short supply in those days.

b) Taking things belonging to other people was quite common.

c) People would freely help out their neighbours if they needed something.

2 *'... if anybody attacked an old person or a kid, the gangs at the street ... the big chaps, you know the corner fellows, got a hold of them.'*

a) Violent attacks on children and the elderly often occurred.

b) Weaker members of the community would be protected by others, even by men who could themselves be violent.

c) Unemployed men hung around the streets looking for trouble.

3 *'And if ye had children, they didnae play oot in the street. They played in the back court.'*

a) Play parks and other facilities for children were inadequate.

b) Children were seen as a nuisance.

c) Children played near where they lived and where they were safe.

↗ Taking it further

Below are some suggestions for research projects, going into issues raised by the extract in more depth.

Oral history

Until relatively recently, 'history' was seen as being concerned with political movements, economic trends, wars and empires and so on. Some historians, however, are interested in researching the everyday lives of ordinary people who may not figure individually in major political or military events.

One early example of this was the Mass Observation project of the 1930s and 1940s, an invaluable source of information on people's opinions during the Second World War, based on volunteers who kept diaries and answered questionnaires.

You could conduct your own 'mass observation' survey by asking people of various ages, occupations and backgrounds about their opinions on certain matters. Possible topics for research might be:

- the differences between your generation and your grandparents' generation
- how socialising has changed
- how technology has changed
- fashion then and now
- football then and now.

Alternatively, you might have a conversation with a grandparent or elderly neighbour, writing down or perhaps recording their memories of how the world has changed in their lifetime, rather like the research carried out by Professor Jean Faley. Time passes and people grow older, making it increasingly important to chronicle ordinary people's experiences before these are lost for ever.

Use the basis of your findings to produce a piece of writing such as a report or personal essay.

Slang

Another area worth researching is the development of slang, which is constantly changing. Every generation has its own slang expressions, which quickly go out of date and give way to new ones. More recent means of communication such as mobile phones and the internet have led to the development of new forms of slang and abbreviations, which young people use constantly and which adults often cannot understand. (An example can be found on page 5.)

This, of course, is part of the reason why language develops as it does. A lexicographer (i.e. a person who compiles a dictionary) once compiled a list of fifteen reasons why people use slang. Here are a few of them:

- To induce either friendliness or intimacy of a deep or a durable kind.
- To show that one belongs to a certain school, trade, or profession, artistic or intellectual set, or social class; in brief, to be 'in the swim' or to establish contact.
- Hence, to show or prove that someone is not 'in the swim'.
- To be secret – not understood by those around one. Children, students, lovers, members of political secret societies, and criminals in or out of prison, are the chief exponents.

Some of these reasons lie behind the kind of expressions and abbreviations used by younger people on the internet today – but it might interest you to know that the above reasons date back to 1934!

- How does language change and develop?
- How do different groups of people identify themselves by the kind of slang they use?
- Why do people use slang?

    Issues such as these would make an interesting research project. Your findings could be presented to your class in the form of a talk or PowerPoint presentation, or could be written up as a report or discursive essay.

Dialect

Some of the differences between formal and informal register were explained following the interview with Daniel Craig. The tenements extract shows another aspect of informal, spoken language: dialect. Dialect is the variety or form of a language used in a particular town or region – in this extract words such as 'ye', 'didnae' and 'oot' are variations of standard English used in Glasgow. Dialect can also involve completely different words that people from a different area might not understand. You might, for example, need to ask an older person from Glasgow to explain to you what is meant by 'a wee daft check key'.

Dialect can be found in practically every part of the British Isles:

- 'I'll do it missen' (I'll do it myself) and ''e nivver said nowt' (he never said anything) are examples of Yorkshire dialect. The Scouse accent and dialect is associated with Merseyside, while people in the Newcastle area have a Geordie accent and dialect.

- Cockney rhyming slang is used in part of London, e.g. Adam and Eve (believe) as in 'I couldn't Adam and Eve it!'; bees and honey (money) as in 'Give us the honey'; apples and pears (stairs) and so on.

- Poet Benjamin Zephaniah, born in Birmingham in 1958, uses vocabulary and rhythms drawn from Jamaican Creole:

I love me mudder and me mudder love me

we come so far from over de sea

we heard dat de streets were paved wid gold

some time it hot, some time it cold

◆ Do you know anyone who speaks with a strong dialect? Talk to them and collect some typical examples and explain them to the class.

Word games

This word square contains eight of the more formal words used in the passage and two of the more informal, dialect forms. Find them using the clues below.

N	P	V	I	V	T	N	E	U	Q	O	L	E	L	J
E	S	T	A	R	K	N	S	N	T	U	C	G	L	V
M	A	N	I	F	E	S	T	A	T	I	O	N	E	W
C	Y	E	G	T	O	K	O	V	Z	O	M	O	P	D
Z	T	R	W	E	F	E	G	L	T	Z	M	V	I	U
H	I	E	T	S	W	T	D	E	N	N	U	N	T	B
B	I	T	X	T	F	J	Z	L	E	K	N	K	O	W
Q	G	V	L	I	L	Z	X	B	M	Y	I	U	M	H
Z	D	I	T	M	P	R	R	A	E	E	T	F	I	C
U	O	U	R	O	D	W	G	I	N	R	Y	V	S	E
X	T	E	V	N	T	T	T	C	E	S	L	Y	E	Z
A	I	J	B	Y	K	K	Z	O	T	Z	Z	U	U	E
R	Q	K	Z	I	H	S	S	S	F	T	F	S	J	K
L	V	E	A	I	F	W	J	S	O	E	R	K	H	P
P	E	F	Q	Q	W	L	C	O	Y	R	C	P	K	B

a) To sum up or represent: E _ _ _ _ _ _ _ _

b) The quality of being friendly and mixing with people: S _ _ _ _ _ _ _

c) Fluent, expressed, articulate, powerfully-expressed: E _ _ _ _ _ _ _

d) Evidence, account of personal experience: T _ _ _ _ _ _ _ _

e) Out (dialect form): _ _ _

f) Type of house divided up into apartments: T _ _ _ _ _ _ _

g) Social grouping of people who have a sense of belonging together: C _ _ _ _ _ _ _ _ _

h) Your (dialect form): _ _ _

i) An outward demonstration of: M _ _ _ _ _ _ _ _ _ _ _ N

j) Noticeable, clearly evident: S _ _ _ _

◆ Now copy and complete the table below to review your progress.

Progress review	Yes
I can identify the differences between formal and informal language.	
I can identify examples of slang and dialect.	
I can recognise examples of jargon.	
I can comment on how an author uses evidence to back up statements.	
I can understand how speakers use anecdote to illustrate their points.	

Chapter 5

Non-verbal communication

Body language

One American 'relationship expert' has estimated that in a conversation between two people 93% of the communication is non-verbal. While it may be difficult to see how such a precise figure can be arrived at, there is no doubt that our tone of voice, manner, posture, hand gestures and facial expressions have as much to do with how someone responds to us as the actual words we speak.

The following extract comes from a book called *Body Language at Work* by Peter Clayton, a management trainer who has studied the way body language affects how people in business deal with colleagues and customers. The book aims to 'reveal the secrets of body language to help you deal confidently with any work situation'. In this extract, Clayton analyses how body language affects someone's performance during a job interview.

The interview

Alice really wants this job. She's been unable to relax for days before the interview. The interviewer, John, cannot know this. All he sees is that Alice presents herself at the interview in a tense, anxious state. John's problem is to decide how much Alice's body language arises from an understandable nervousness about the interview process, and how much from defensiveness – a desire to cover up weaknesses. If John gives her too hard a time, the chances are that he'll learn even less of the truth than he otherwise would do.

I Nervous start

Alice (see left) looks tense and defensive. Her upright position, with legs tucked under the seat, arms straight, and hands clasped between her legs, are all body language trouble spots. There is no way of telling at this stage whether she is merely nervous or has things to hide. John's only option is to be patient and to let her unwind in her own time. Note the position of Alice's feet (left). They have now moved forward slightly, but even so, they are still nervously tight to the chair.

2 Settling down?

John's training as an interviewer has taught him to do the obvious in a situation like this (see right). He gives Alice some background about what sort of company she's hoping to join, bringing in anecdotes from the last sales conference, with one or two designed to make her laugh. He hands her a brochure that illustrates a point he's making, so that in receiving it, she has to move forward. Just a small gesture such as this can speed the calming process when someone is genuinely nervous. John should now be looking to see if Alice's feet come involuntarily forward from under the seat. If so, this would confirm that she's starting to settle down.

3 Going better

Some minutes later, Alice has realised that the interview is less frightening than she had expected (see left). Her body language has softened accordingly. The arms are no longer forming a tight defensive barrier and the feet have strayed out from under the chair. There is even some mirroring behaviour: Alice is unconsciously echoing John's crossed legs and pointing foot. So far so good. There seems to be little doubt that her tight body language was just down to nervousness.

4 Talking turkey

Once John has seen Alice's body language starting to soften, he uses the standard interviewing technique of mixing questions that will help him assess how Alice has succeeded in her current job, and how she would cope in her new position.

John now starts to ask some specific questions. He wants to know what Alice did to improve the credit control system she worked on and how she measured her effect. The questions seem to touch a raw nerve: Alice's legs move backwards, the head drops a little and the hands are folded into a tight barrier, all suggesting defensiveness and concealment. John needs to know exactly why she is feeling uncomfortable, but wisely accepts that having invested so much time getting Alice to open up, it would be self-defeating to press the point.

John now asks Alice to tell him what she thinks were her best achievements in running her department. Again, the feet drift forwards and the hands loosen up. Having heard Alice's answer, John decides quite quickly that she'll be OK for the post and hints at this, without saying it directly. Before Alice's body language can change, however, he reverts to the credit control question, asking her what part she played and how she felt about it.

5 Flashback

Alice is biting her bottom lip and stroking her chin – both gestures indicating that she's trying to make up her mind about what to say. As she explains how poorly the project was handled, and how she had disagreed with the results, John is pleased to see that her pupils are slightly raised and that they are moving

from left to right and back again. This is typical of people who are recalling events as they actually happened – their eyes are 'seeing' the events as pictures that go with the words. She is confirming her own story as she relates it.

Broadly speaking, right-handed people's pupils have a tendency to move from left to right when they are recalling events as they happened; left-handers' pupils move right to left.

6 Home straight

John now says, 'Well I can understand why you're looking for a new job – seems a sensible move to me.' Alice's body language again opens up, confirming she's at ease with the situation and with John's opinion of her. Her body language is closely mirroring John's – particularly the position of the hands, first in the lap, then extending forward towards the knee. These are strong signs that she approves of John because she feels he has assessed her fairly.

⊕ *Taking a closer look*

1 The writer identifies six stages in this interview, during which the different feelings of the job applicant, Alice, are demonstrated through her body language. At most stages of the interview we are also told how the interviewer, John, responds to Alice's body language.

What do the following examples of body language show about either John's or Alice's feelings about how the interview is going? Copy the table below and fill in the empty gaps. One example has been done for you.

Body language	What it shows
Alice tucks her legs under the seat and clasps her hands between her legs.	Alice is initially tense and defensive.
John hands Alice a brochure.	
	Alice has realised the interview is less frightening than she expected.
Alice is biting her bottom lip and stroking her chin.	
By the end of the interview Alice's body language closely mirrors John's.	

2 *For discussion:* look at columns A and B below. Column A is a list of aspects of body language, while column B is a list of what this body language reveals about a person.

Discuss these in pairs or groups, and match up each item in column A with a suitable explanation from column B.

A

1 arms crossed
2 tapping fingers
3 biting lip
4 staring directly at the other person for some time
5 looking down
6 weak handshake
7 straight, upright stance
8 palms of hands open outwards
9 head tilted to one side
10 stroking chin or pulling at ear lobe
11 pupils of eyes dilated (enlarged)

B

1 attempt to dominate or intimidate the other person
2 defensive attitude: creating a barrier
3 bored and impatient
4 showing interest in what the other person is saying
5 lack of self-confidence; unenthusiastic attitude
6 strong and self-assured
7 indecisiveness
8 strong liking for the other person
9 openness, honesty and sincerity
10 nervousness; being unsure of what to say
11 shyness; uncertainty; possible attempt to hide something

3 *For discussion:* Look at the pictures overleaf. Write down what you feel the expression or body language conveys about each person's character, attitudes or feelings. Then compare notes in pairs or groups. To what extent did everyone agree?

4 Script and act out (or simply improvise) a situation, using body language as well as spoken words to convey the person's feelings. You could, for example, choose a situation where a new student joins a social group at lunch break for the first time or a new employee sits down at a work meeting for the first time; equally, you might be able to think of another scenario of your own. The photos above may also give you some inspiration.

🔧 Tools of the trade: layout and presentation

While this extract can be read as a series of consecutive paragraphs, it depends on other features of layout and presentation for its impact including:

● use of illustrations

● division into sections

● use of sub-headings.

For discussion: why are these features particularly suited to the topic being discussed?

🔧 Tools of the trade: summarising skills

A key English skill is the ability to summarise a section of a passage, or the whole extract. Here are some guidelines on acquiring the necessary skills:

● Distinguish between main points and the evidence/explanations that expand upon/ back up these points.

● Include only the main points; omit the detailed examples. If, for example, there are some statistics, quotations or anecdotes (stories to illustrate a point) these should not be included in the summary.

● Stick to the facts of what the writer is saying; don't include your own opinions or response. There should be nothing in the summary that was not mentioned in the original passage. In other words, adopt an **impersonal** stance.

● Do not number points or use sub-headings (even if, as in the case of the body language extract, they are used in the original passage). However, if you have time, it is a good idea to do a draft of your summary and jot down in note form, with or without bullet-points, the main things you are going to include.

● Your summary should consist of ONE paragraph only. In some cases, you may be given a word limit.

● It is usually better to write the summary in the past tense, even if the original passage is in the present.

● The summary can be made to flow by using linking words and phrases at the start of sentences, such as 'however', 'furthermore', 'in addition to', 'similarly', 'as a result' and 'consequently'.

● Paraphrase the writer's points. This means you should express them in your own words to some extent – it is all right to use some of the writer's words but you should not copy out whole sentences word for word.

Points and evidence

In order to distinguish between main points and back-up explanations, you need to understand something about sentence structure and paragraph construction. Often, but not always, there will be one sentence (perhaps the first one) that states the main idea developed in the rest of the paragraph. Look, for instance, at the structure of the first paragraph of the introduction to the extract on interviews.

'Alice really wants this job. She's been unable to relax for days before the interview. The interviewer, John, cannot know this. All he sees is that Alice presents herself at the interview in a tense, anxious state.'

Main point (topic sentence):

Alice really wants this job.

↓

Evidence:

She's been unable to relax for days before the interview.

↓

Second point, arising out of the first one:

The interviewer, John, cannot know this.

↓

Evidence:

All he sees is that Alice presents herself at the interview in a tense, anxious state.

✎ For practice

Copy the table below and decide which of the following are main points and which are evidence or examples.

		Main point	Evidence
1	John starts to ask some specific questions.		
2	One of the things John wanted to know was what Alice did to improve the credit control system she worked on and how she measured her effect.		
3	Alice's body language at the interview showed how nervous she felt.		
4	At one stage, Alice's legs moved backwards, her head dropped a little and her hands were folded into a tighter barrier.		
5	John was a skilled interviewer.		
6	In the course of the interview Alice's body language softened.		
7	Her arms were no longer forming a tight defensive barrier and her feet had strayed out from under the chair.		
8	The change in the position of her hands, from being in her lap to extending forwards towards her knees, was a strong sign she approves of John because she felt he had treated her fairly.		
9	Alice began to mirror John's behaviour.		

Writing the summary

Now write a summary of the whole interview, identifying the six different stages without giving all the detailed examples. Remember that the summary should be a single paragraph, without sub-headings. The first section ('Nervous start') has been done to start you off. You should be able to summarise the main points of the whole passage in no more than 120 words (including the 28 used here to start you off!).

At the start of the interview Alice's body language revealed that she was tense and defensive. John therefore decided to be patient and wait for her to relax. ...

Consolidate your knowledge

◆ You have 1 minute to explain to the person sitting beside you how to go about writing a summary.

Word games

Match up the words in the box with a suitable definition.

1 A story used to illustrate a point: _ _ _ _ _ _ _ _

2 Taking up a position of self-protection: _ _ _ _ _ _ _ _ _

3 Unintentionally, done without realising it: _ _ _ _ _ _ _ _ _ _ _

4 Body movement, particularly the hands: _ _ _ _ _ _ _

5 To estimate or measure: _ _ _ _ _ _

6 To prove, back up or establish: _ _ _ _ _ _ _

7 An inclination to: _ _ _ _ _ _ _ _

| gesture | assess | involuntary | anecdote | tendency | defensive | confirm |

◆ Now copy and complete the table below to review your progress.

Progress review	Yes
I can recognise the difference between statements and evidence.	
I can recognise how body language can indicate how a person is feeling.	
I can identify the main points of a passage.	

Chapter 6
Fiction and non-fiction

Techniques for writing fiction and non-fiction

Writers use different techniques for fiction and non-fiction. The two passages in this chapter, both on the topic of haunted houses, illustrate this.

◆ Below is a list of some of the features that may distinguish the two genres. Draw up a table with two columns, headed 'Fiction' and 'Non-fiction'. Enter each feature in the appropriate column. For example, if you think that 'Plot develops, with a beginning, middle and end' is typical of fiction, enter this feature in the column headed 'Fiction'. There are ten features for fiction, and ten for non-fiction. Copying out the features will help you to remember them.

1 Plot develops, with a beginning, middle and end.
2 The topic is some aspect of the real world.
3 Actions and events have been invented.
4 No attempt to create a mood.
5 Constructed, invented conversations.
6 An argument advances logically, with links between the various stages.
7 Descriptive language builds up a mood.
8 The tone is neutral or impersonal.
9 Few facts and figures, though setting may be a date in real time.
10 Figurative language (similes and metaphors).
11 Argument reaches a conclusion or summing up.
12 References are made to real places.
13 The characters are invented.
14 Language is simple and non-figurative (lacking similes and metaphors).
15 Plot ends with a solution or denouement.
16 Precise facts, figures, statistics.
17 Comments that real people have actually said are included.
18 Imaginary settings.
19 References are made to real people and real actions.
20 Tone conveys suspense or emotion.

Exceptions

You will find exceptions in the use of these features. For example, although much non-fiction does not focus on mood, a sports journalist describing a real football match may want to create a sense of excitement. Personal non-fiction writing, such as a diary (see page 20 for an example), may have some of the features more usually found in fiction. Fiction sometimes uses real places as settings, and even real people as characters, e.g. *Arthur and George* by Julian Barnes is about the author of Sherlock Holmes, Arthur Conan Doyle.

Passage I: Britain's most haunted houses

Nigel Jones *describes some of the properties visited by presenter Michaela Strachan while researching a television series about Britain's most haunted houses.*

1 They came for the women at dawn. Knowing they would die on the scaffold, the innocents condemned as witches spent a miserable last night in the tiny cottage lock-up called The Cage, chained or strapped to the wall of their cell in utter darkness. But do their restless spirits still horrify those who come to The Cage today?

2 For her new television series, Michaela Strachan visited the property and others like it to find Britain's most haunted house. It was an experience she approached with a healthy dose of scepticism: 'We weren't doing an actual ghost hunt ourselves, but finding out about the ghosts and the history of the places we visited.'

3   The Cage's current owner, Vanessa Mitchell, has no doubt that her property is shared with unseen guests. 'It's the most frightening house in Britain,' she says. 'It's extremely haunted and I can't live there any more – nor can anyone else.' Vanessa and her four-month-old son Jesse were forced out of The Cage by a campaign of spooky phenomena: footsteps, the sound of women and children weeping, cushions thrown through the air and mysterious bloodstains appearing on the floor. 'There have been deaths, suicides, diseases, depression and divorce,' she says of those who have tried – and failed – to live in the tiny 16th-century former jailhouse in the village of St Osyth near Clacton in Essex. 'No one can live there for any length of time, and it regularly goes on sale.'

4   John Chapman, a former tenant, agrees. 'I don't believe in ghosts, but one night I was alone in the house and I heard footsteps climbing the stairs to my bedroom,' he admits. 'Then I saw the door handle actually turning – yet I know there was no one there. After that, I left.'

5   Chris Palmer, a psychic investigator, suffered a more physical ghostly experience – he was pushed down The Cage's stairs by a spook. Chris says, 'We were setting up cameras to take photographs when I felt a violent shove in my back – but there was no one there. Luckily I landed on a colleague and didn't hurt myself.' Now Vanessa only rents The Cage to psychic investigators and short-stay guests. She says, 'They say the dead can't hurt you, but I know they can.'

6   Another Essex place of judgement and punishment is the Old Courthouse Inn in Great Bromley. As its name implies, the former courthouse, which is now a B&B pub, was where criminals were tried – and often taken straight to the gallows. It is haunted by a woman in a maid's uniform, and guests have complained of a feeling of being watched. The pub's ghosts have been caught on camera by spirit snapper Ron Bowers. He's taken scores of photographs there, which have shown shapes witnesses claim were not visible to them.

7   Justice meted out at the Old Courthouse may have been rough but at least it was swift. However, debtors banged up in Derby Gaol languished there for months or years, sometimes driven to suicide by despair. The prison, now a museum run by local historian Richard Felix, also claims to be Britain's most haunted building. Richard says the 'torment and terror of its past lingers in the very fabric' of the building. Visitors to the museum have seen the oak cell doors close on their own, have smelt the scent of roses, felt sick and been pushed and shoved by unseen hands. At a séance held in the gaol, a heavy table pushed a visitor close to a burning fire, and Richard has seen a ghost gliding along the corridor. Richard believes the man in black 19th-century clothes was the unquiet spirit of George Batty, a rapist hanged in 1825 when the jail closed down, or perhaps the spirit of the jail's last warden, Blyth Simpson, who objects to his successor's presence. Richard says, 'He still thinks he runs the place – he resents me terribly.'

8   A genuine victim of injustice – burned alive in 1555 under the Catholic Queen 'Bloody' Mary for preaching his Protestant faith – was George Marsh. The scene of Marsh's trial, 15th-century Smithills Hall in Bolton, Greater Manchester, is haunted by his ghost. Joan Sheppard, a museum tour guide, thinks she's seen him – and felt his rage. Joan says, 'I was in the Green Room where Marsh was questioned, the hall's most haunted chamber, when I saw a man in the mirror. He had white hair and was looking at me. Then something grabbed my wrist and held me so tightly it bruised.' Since then, Joan has been too scared to enter the room alone.

Smithills Hall in Bolton is haunted by the ghost of George Marsh who was burned alive in 1555

9 Not all haunted houses are the sites of sin and suffering, however. Another Bolton museum, the half-timbered Tudor house curiously named 'Hall I' th'Wood', seems to be inhabited by its former owners, the wealthy Brownlow family. But, says ghost hunter Jason Karl, they are fading away with time. 'Where once you could see a whole human form, nowadays all we see is a pair of disembodied legs climbing the stairs or sitting on a bed, accompanied by a sense of oppression or dread.

10 And did Michaela encounter anything that made her a believer? Well, while filming in the Hall her camera crew heard the sound of children playing outside. They went to the window ... but there was no one and nothing to be seen. Spooky, eh?

⊕ *Taking a closer look*

◆ With a partner, look again at the ten features (from the list on page 49) that you identified as typical of **non-fiction**. How many of them can you find in this passage?

◆ Write down the number of each feature you have found. Beside each number, quote or briefly explain one or two pieces of evidence for your answer.

◆ Now answer the questions below.

1 Look again at paragraph 1. Think about how the author has chosen to *begin* this piece of writing. How does the first paragraph relate to the rest of the passage? How does the author create a **link** between the first paragraph and those that follow? Explain the ways in which paragraph 1 is different in both ideas and style from the rest of the passage. **4 marks**

2 Look at all the claims in paragraphs 3–5 that The Cage is haunted. Using your own words as far as possible, sum up how far the evidence seems convincing or unconvincing. (Focus solely on the *evidence*; do not allow your own beliefs to influence your answer.) **4 marks**

3 Look again at paragraphs 6–8. There are claims that The Old Courthouse Inn, Derby Gaol and Smithhills Hall are haunted. Say whether each of the following statements is TRUE or FALSE:

a) Ron Bowers' photographs at the Old Courthouse Inn failed to show anything people had not seen.

b) Visitors to Derby Gaol museum seem to have been put in real danger at times.

c) The museum tour guide at Smithhills Hall claims she is not scared of the 'ghost' there although it grabbed her wrist. **3 marks**

4 Read paragraph 9 again. Compare the way in which 'Hall I' th'Wood' seems to be haunted with the other places mentioned. (Mention any similarities as well as differences.) **3 marks**

'Hall I' th'Wood', Manchester

5 Pick the answer that you think best sums up Michaela Strachan's response to the question in paragraph 10:

a) Michaela didn't believe in any of the ghosts at all.

b) Michaela felt the houses were definitely haunted.

c) Michaela had had one slightly strange experience that she thought *might* be supernatural. **1 mark**

6 'Spooky, eh?' Describe the **tone** and word **choice** used in this sentence. How far do they suggest the writer is convinced by Michaela's story? **3 marks**

A plaque on 'the most haunted house in Britain'

7 This extract appeared in a magazine shortly before a series of programmes was aired on television. Its purpose was to publicise the series and attract viewers. Say how successful you feel the writer has been in achieving this purpose. Refer closely to the passage in your answer. **2 marks**

Total: 20 marks

Tools of the trade

Structure

In a non-fiction piece of writing, writers arrange their ideas carefully so that they unfold in a logical way.

● Can you work out the arrangement of the writer's ideas in this passage? Copy and complete the table below. One section is done for you.

Paragraph 1	
Paragraph 2	
Paragraphs 3, 4 and 5	
Paragraphs 6, 7, 8 and 9	Four more examples of allegedly 'haunted' buildings are explored, one in each paragraph, ending with a slightly different one.
Paragraph 10	

Linkage

The writer must **link** the ideas in a piece of writing, so that the reader is guided smoothly and logically from one to the next.

◆ In paragraph 1 the writer uses **a question** to link it to the next stage of the argument. He then goes on to answer the question. Can you find another example of this technique later in the extract?

◆ Paragraphs 3, 4 and 5 link together as they all start in the same way. What is this way?

◆ In paragraph 6, the writer uses a simple link: the word 'another' introduces the next building to be discussed. Can you find a second example of this in a later paragraph?

● Sometimes a whole sentence or pair of sentences acts as a link. Look at this example.

'Justice meted out at the Old Courthouse may have been rough but at least it was swift. However, debtors banged up in Derby Gaol languished there for months or years.'

The phrase 'Old Courthouse' links back to the place described in paragraph 6 and the idea of 'justice' that was 'swift' refers to the people who were hanged. The adverb 'however' shows that something different is about to come up. He then introduces his next topic, 'Derby Gaol', and the plight of people who were kept there for 'months or years'. This will be expanded on in the next part of the passage.

◆ The first sentence of paragraph 9 is: 'Not all haunted houses are the sites of sin and suffering, however.' Can you show how this sentence acts as a link in a similar way by filling in the blanks on the following page (the correct number of letters in each word required are given as a clue)?

The phrase '_ _ _ _ _ / _ _ / _ _ _ / _ _ _ / _ _ _ _ _ _ _ _ _' links back to the examples he has just discussed, while '_ _ _ / _ _ _ / _ _ _ _ _ _ _ / _ _ _ _ _ _' links on to the next example to be discussed, which is *not* a site of sin and suffering. The adverb '_ _ _ _ _ _ _' also prepares the reader for a change.

Word games

Choose a word from the box below that best fits the definition. All of the words were used in passage 1.

1 separate from a body/without a body attached: _ _ _ _ _ _ _ _ _ _ _ _

2 unwillingness to believe; distrust: _ _ _ _ _ _ _ _ _ _

3 measured out; dispensed: _ _ _ _ _ / _ _ _

4 pined away: _ _ _ _ _ _ _ _ _

5 people who owe money: _ _ _ _ _ _ _

6 meeting at which people attempt to contact the spirits of the dead: _ _ _ _ _ _

7 framework on which people are hanged: _ _ _ _ _ _ _

8 strange happenings; apparitions: _ _ _ _ _ _ _ _ _

> scepticism   meted out   séance   phenomena   gallows   debtors   disembodied   languished

Passage 2: A night in a haunted house

This second extract is adapted from the opening of The Haunters and The Haunted *by Edward Bulwer-Lytton, a nineteenth-century writer. The narrator is preparing to spend the night in a house in London, after a friend has aroused his curiosity by telling him it is haunted.*

1 About half-past nine, I strolled towards the haunted house. Earlier in the day I had given my servant the keys, instructing him to light fires and air the beds. I took with me a favourite dog – an exceedingly sharp, bold, and vigilant bull-terrier – a dog fond of prowling about strange passages at night in search of rats – a dog of dogs for a ghost.

2 I reached the house, knocked, and my servant opened the door with a cheerful smile. 'All right, sir. Very comfortable.'

'Oh,' I said, rather disappointed; 'have you not seen or heard anything remarkable?'

'Well, sir, I have heard something – the sound of feet pattering behind me; and once or twice small noises like whispers close at my ear – nothing more.'

'You were not at all frightened?'

'Not a bit, sir'; and the man's bold look reassured me that whatever might happen he would not desert me.

3   We were in the hall, the street door closed, and my attention was now drawn to my dog. He had at first run in eagerly enough, but had sneaked back to the door, and was scratching and whining to get out. After patting him on the head and encouraging him gently, the dog seemed to reconcile himself to the situation and followed me through the house, but keeping close at my heels instead of hurrying inquisitively in advance, which was his usual habit in all strange places.

4   After looking all around the house with my servant, I went to my bedroom. The room he had selected for me was a large one with two windows fronting the street. The bed was opposite to the fire, which he had lit; a door in the wall to the left, between the bed and the window, led into the room which the man had chosen for himself. This was a small room which had no exit onto the landing, and no other door but the one which connected it to the bedroom I was to occupy.

5   I read quietly enough till about half-past eleven. I then threw myself dressed on the bed and told my man he could go to his own room, but must keep himself awake. I told him to leave open the door between the two rooms. Thus alone, I kept two candles burning on the table by my bed-head. I placed my watch beside them and calmly resumed my book.

6   Opposite to me the fire burned bright and clear, and on the hearth-rug, seemingly asleep, lay the dog. In about twenty minutes I felt an exceedingly cold air pass by my cheek, like a sudden draught. I thought the door to my right onto the landing must have got open; but no, it was closed. I then turned my glance to my left and saw the flame of the candles violently swayed as if by a wind. At the same moment the watch slid from the table – softly, softly – no visible hand – it was gone. I sprang up and looked round the floor – no sign of the watch. Three slow, loud, distinct knocks were now heard at the bed-head; my servant called out, 'Is that you, sir?'

'No, be on your guard.'

7   The dog now roused himself and sat on his haunches, his ears moving quickly backwards and forwards. He kept his eyes fixed on me with a look so strange that he concentrated all my attention on himself. Slowly he rose up, all his hair bristling, and stood perfectly rigid, and with the same wild stare. I had no time, however, to examine the dog. My servant emerged from his room; and if ever I saw horror in the human face, it was then. I should not have recognised him had we met in the street, so altered was every feature. He passed by me quickly, saying in a whisper that seemed scarcely to come from his lips, 'Run – run! It is after me.' He reached the door to the landing, pulled it open and rushed out. I followed him onto the landing, calling him to stop; but, without heeding me, he bounded down the stairs, clinging to the bannisters and taking several steps at a time. I heard, where I stood, the street door open – heard it again clap shut. I was left alone in the haunted house.

8   It was but for a moment that I remained undecided whether or not to follow my servant; pride and curiosity alike forbade so cowardly a flight. I re-entered my room, closing the door after me, and proceeded cautiously into the inner room. I found nothing to justify my servant's terror. I carefully examined the walls, to see if there were any concealed door. I could find no trace of one – not even a seam in the dull brown paper with which the room was hung. How, then, had the Thing, whatever it was, which had so scared him, obtained access except through my own room?

9   I returned to my room, shut and locked the door that opened upon the interior one, and stood on the hearth, expectant and prepared. I now perceived that the dog had slunk into an angle of the wall, and was pressing himself close against it, as if literally trying to force his way into it. I approached the animal and spoke to it; the poor brute was evidently beside itself with terror. It showed all its teeth, the slaver dropping from its jaws, and would certainly have bitten me if I had touched it. It did not seem to recognise me. Whoever has seen at the zoo a rabbit fascinated by a snake, and cowering in a corner, may form some idea of the anguish which the dog exhibited.

10 I am unwilling to believe in the supernatural, and was still sure that all I had witnessed was caused by someone as mortal as myself. In order to calm my imagination, I turned again to my book, and riveted eye and thought on its pages. I now became aware that something interposed between the page and the light – the page was overshadowed; I looked up, and saw what I shall find it very difficult, perhaps impossible to describe. It was a Darkness shaping itself out of the air in very undefined outline. I cannot say it was of a human form, and yet it had more resemblance to a human form, or rather shadow, than anything else. While I gazed, a feeling of intense cold seized me. And now, to add to my horror, the light began slowly to wane from the candles; it was the same with the fire – the light was extracted from the fuel; in a few minutes the room was in utter darkness.

Bull terrier

⊕ Taking a closer look

◆ With a partner, look again at the ten features (from the list on page 49) that you identified as typical of **fiction**. How many of them can you find in this passage?

◆ Write the number of each feature you have found down the margin. Beside each number, quote or briefly explain one or two pieces of evidence for your answer.

Language change

There is another difference between the two passages. The first was written this century, whereas the second was written in 1859. Certain details, such as the candles and the fact that the narrator has a servant, tell us that the setting of the second is not the present day. The language itself is also a little different to what a writer would use now, although it is still quite easy to

Extract from a 19th-century book

understand. The word **archaic** is used for such old-fashioned language. For example:

● The writer uses fewer abbreviations than we would today. 'Have you not seen or heard anything remarkable?'

● Some individual words and expressions are old-fashioned: 'forbade'; 'Be on your guard.'

● Sentence structures are slightly more complex: 'It was but for a moment I remained undecided…'.

● The language is more formal in tone than a modern writer would use: 'I now became aware that something interposed between the page and the light…'.

◆ Can you translate the examples given here into the English we use today?

◆ Choose one other example of **archaic** language from the extract and translate it into modern English. Compare your example with others in your class or group.

◆ Now answer the following questions, which will help you appreciate the writer's craft in creating suspense:

1 In paragraph 1, the writer describes the dog in detail. What is the value of this later in the story? How does the focus on the dog throughout the extract help build suspense? **4 marks**

2 In paragraph 2, the **character** of the servant is made clear through the dialogue. What impression do we get of the servant here, and how does the servant's role in the rest of the story build suspense? **4 marks**

3 The narrator **contrasts** with the servant and the dog by remaining calm. Show how the writer achieves this impression in his presentation of the narrator, and explain if you think this increases or decreases the suspense. **4 marks**

4 Ghost stories have been a popular genre for hundreds of years. However, in recent years, readers have tended to find them ridiculous. Say how far you think this example, written over 100 years ago, would or would not manage to grip a modern reader. (Your answer may take into account the fact that a series of television programmes on haunted houses is being made.) **3 marks**

Tools of the trade

Suspense

The purpose of a ghost story is to entertain the reader. Many people enjoy being scared from the safety of their armchair. The writer must build up suspense so that the reader is gripped by the tension.

One technique that Bulwer-Lytton has used is to focus firstly on the behaviour of the dog, and then on that of the servant. He describes the terror of these two characters (here we can consider the dog a character) and this builds suspense as we wonder why a brave dog and a cheerful, well-balanced man should be scared out of their wits like this. The fact that we do not know what has frightened them racks up the tension.

Another technique Bulwer-Lytton uses is to give a lot of down-to-earth, ordinary details of the house (see paragraphs 4 and 8 especially). This attention to mundane things, such as the position of doors and windows, builds realism and contrasts dramatically with the exciting supernatural happenings.

Taking it further

◆ Try writing a ghost story of your own. You could use some of the techniques you have observed in Bulwer-Lytton's story.

◆ If you think you might enjoy reading a ghost story, you could try one of the following:

◆ *The Woman in Black* by Susan Hill: a solicitor is sent to the haunted Eel Marsh

House to sort out the papers of its owner who has just died.

◆ *The Mist in the Mirror* by Susan Hill: a young man finds strange happenings at a school when he goes there to investigate a ghost story.

◆ *The Turn of the Screw* by Henry James: a difficult but rewarding story about two small children who appear to be possessed by the spirits of a pair of evil servants who used to work at the house.

For practice

The Arctic convoys

The two passages below describe the Arctic convoys of the Second World War, when British ships attempted to deliver war materials to the Russian ports within the Arctic Circle. Many ships were sunk and many men died as a result of both terrible weather and enemy action.

◆ One of the passages is fiction, the other non-fiction. Can you tell which is which? Read both passages, and then do the tasks that follow. This could be done in small groups.

Passage 1

1 The equation of risk for the Arctic convoys was grim. During the winter the ice, extending southward, obliged them to pass within two or three hundred miles of German-held territory. The summer route was further north and therefore further away from the German airfields, but the daylight was perpetual. The winter convoys had to pass dangerously close to German bases. The summer ones were exposed twenty-four hours a day to German air attack for at least one third of the voyage.

2 The convoys to north Russia began sailing in September 1941. The first twelve arrived safely. But PQ13, as the thirteenth convoy was code-named, lost two ships out of nineteen; PQ15 lost three ships and PQ16 lost seven. The north Russia convoys were obviously becoming increasingly risky. Churchill, nevertheless, was determined to do all he could to help the Russians.

3 The thirty-six merchant ships of PQ17, a larger convoy than its predecessors, sailed for Archangel in June 1942. The Germans located PQ17 from the air on 1 July, and air attacks began on 4 July. Misled by false intelligence that the German battleship *Tirpitz* was approaching, the Admiralty ordered the escort of PQ17 to return westward and the convoy itself to scatter. The Admiralty had decided in advance that the escort vessels which accompanied the convoys were more valuable than the convoys themselves. Obeying orders that could not be questioned, the escort retired and the convoy was massacred by German aircraft. Twenty-four ships were sunk. Some of the others were beached. A few struggled on to Archangel.

Passage 2

1 The cold was now intense. To keep a watch, especially a watch on the bridge, was torture: the first shock of that bitter wind seared the lungs, left a man fighting for breath: if he had forgotten to don gloves – first the silk gloves, then the woollen mittens, then the sheepskin gauntlets – and touched a handrail, the palms of the hands seared off, the skin burnt as by white-hot metal. On the bridge, the deadly chill crept upwards from feet to calves to thighs, nose and chin turned white with frostbite and demanded immediate attention, and then, by far the worst of all, the end of the watch, the return below deck, the excruciating agony of returning circulation.

2 But all these things were relative trifles, personal inconveniences to be shrugged aside. The real danger lay elsewhere, in the fact of ice. The danger lay in its weight. The escort carriers and the destroyers were vulnerable, terribly so. The carriers, already unstable with the great height and weight of their reinforced flight-decks, provided a huge, smooth, flat surface to the falling snow, ideal conditions for the formation of ice. Earlier on, it had been possible to keep the flight-decks relatively clear – working parties had toiled incessantly with brooms and sledges, salt and steam hoses. But the weather had deteriorated so badly now that to send out a man on that wildly pitching, staggering flight-deck, glassy and infinitely treacherous, would be to send him to his death.

3   Two hours passed, two hours in which the temperature fell to zero, hesitated, then shrank steadily beyond it, two hours in which the barometer tumbled after it. The squadron presented a fantastic picture now, little toy-boats of sugar-icing, dazzling white, gleaming and sparkling in the pale, winter sunshine, pitching crazily through the ever-lengthening, ever-deepening valleys of grey and green of the cold Norwegian Sea.

4   Rear-Admiral Tyndall saw nothing beautiful about it. A man who was wont to claim that he never worried, he was seriously troubled now. 'What on earth persuaded me to become a squadron commander?' he muttered.

◆ For each passage, make a list of bullet points, based on the checklist on page 49, noting which features are present.

◆ Decide which passage is fiction and which non-fiction, giving your reasons.

◆ Did you notice the non-fiction passage had some style features typical of fiction, and the fiction passage had some features typical of non-fiction? Which are these?

◆ Write a short essay on ONE of the passages, referring closely to the text and including brief quotations, analysing the features that make the writing effective.

🔧 Tools of the trade

Word choice: connotation and denotation

These terms express two aspects of meaning. *Denotation* is the **literal** meaning of a word, while *connotation* refers to the **associations** that the word has. For example, the literal meaning of the word 'rat' is a small mammal. That is the simple **denotation** of the word.

However, 'rat' has many '**connotations**' or associations. It is associated with treachery and disloyalty, as in the phrase 'rats desert a sinking ship'. From this connotation it has become a verb: 'to rat' on someone means to betray him or her. In the case of the word 'rat', the connotations are all negative. Rats are known to live in sewers and rubbish dumps and to spread plague and disease.

Connotation is a useful word to use in your analysis, as it is often the key to a writer's **tone** or to the **mood** a writer creates. Very often, the connotations of a word will be **emotive**: conveying and/or arousing emotion. Rats arouse emotions of disgust, hatred, fear and disapproval.

Example

Look again at passage 1 on the Arctic convoys (pages 57–58).

In paragraph 3, the writer builds up to the story of how convoy PQ17 was almost completely destroyed. After explaining that the Admiralty ordered the warships escorting the merchant ships to withdraw as they were too valuable to lose, the writer says the merchantmen were then '*massacred*' by the German bombers. A 'massacre' has connotations of cruelty on a massive scale inflicted on defenceless victims. By choosing to express it **emotively,** rather than in a more neutral way, such as 'many ships were sunk', the writer conveys his indignation that the Admiralty left these ships to their fate, and simultaneously arouses a sense of outrage in the reader.

✎ For practice

Copy the table below. For each of the denotations, say what **connotations** the word has, and whether these are **positive** or **negative** (sometimes you may find both). Think of common sayings that include these words. Where appropriate, try also to explain the **emotive** impact of the connotations.

Denotation	Connotation
1 the colour green	
2 the colour blue	
3 sheep/lambs	
4 snake	
5 shark	
6 apple	
7 fire	
8 milk	

Remember that a writer's word choice can shape the reader's response because of the connotations aroused. For example, a political writer on the topic of immigration may choose between the terms 'illegal immigrant' and 'asylum seeker'.

◆ In this case, how would the choice of term affect the message? What would it reveal about the writer's attitude to the person referred to?

English is a language rich in **synonyms**. A dictionary definition of **synonym** is 'a word having the same meaning as another; a word that can be used as an alternative'.

However, there are always subtle differences between words that govern a writer's choice. The **connotations** of a word will determine whether its effect is **positive** or **negative**. Words denoting degrees of generosity and meanness illustrate this clearly.

◆ Look at the following list of words. Decide what the **connotations** of each word are, and then rank them in order of **positive/ negative** effect.

1   generous; spendthrift; lavish; liberal; free-spending; wasteful; open-handed

2   mean; economical; stingy; thrifty; miserly; careful; tight-fisted

Figurative language and imagery: simile and metaphor

It is useful to look at imagery at this point, as many connotations are in the form of metaphor. For example, the word 'rat' is used as a metaphor for a treacherous, despicable person. Since a rat is a disgusting animal found in sewers and rubbish dumps it becomes a suitable image for a person we despise. Both **simile** and **metaphor** are types of comparison that writers use to give a clearer impression of their ideas. The **image** is the thing the idea is being compared to. The word **imagery** refers to all the images used by the writer.

Technically speaking, **similes** are introduced by 'like', 'as' or 'as if', whereas **metaphors** simply say one thing *is* another. **Personification**, where things are spoken of as if they are alive, is a form of metaphor. Writers frequently use imagery when trying to describe things or put over a point of view in a striking, memorable manner. It is more common in fiction, but non-fiction writers also use this technique.

In the passage on haunted houses at the beginning of this chapter (pages 49–51), we are told Michaela Strachan approached the accounts of haunting with 'a healthy dose' of distrust. The image here is of taking a dose of medicine, which will inoculate her against being too gullible, so that she will not 'swallow' (to use another metaphor) all the tales.

Note: a phrase introduced by 'like' isn't *always* a simile.

To be a real simile, the image must be both *like* and *unlike* the thing – it cannot actually *be* the thing. For example, in the passage on pages 53–55 about the man spending the night in a haunted house, we hear of 'small noises like whispers', and the cold air being 'like a sudden draught'. These are *not* true similes since the noises *could be* whispers, and the cold air *could be* just a draught.

Look at the example below of a true simile. It is taken from a short story called *Through the Tunnel* by Doris Lessing.

'There she was, a speck of yellow under an umbrella that looked like a slice of orange peel.'

Look first at the ways in which an umbrella is *not* like a slice of orange peel.

Umbrella	Slice of orange peel
Very large	Quite small
Made of fabric or plastic	Organic, part of a fruit
Man-made	Naturally growing

But, they *are* also *alike*, both being:

- orange coloured
- the same shape, a gently curved wedge
- apparently the same size – since the large beach umbrella is being viewed from a distance it will look as tiny as a piece of orange peel

The simile is effective as it conjures up the image in our mind's eye because of these three similarities.

Think also of the **connotations** of orange peel (or the orange it comes from): it is sweet to taste and smell, and is therefore an attractive image appealing to these senses, as well as just visually appropriate. Oranges are healthy and nutritious, and these connotations build up a very positive, pleasant image.

When you are discussing imagery in a language question, it is important to:

1. Identify the **object of the image** (in this case orange peel).
2. Discuss the **points of similarity** and also any **connotations** the object itself may have (here: sweet smell, taste and health-giving properties).
3. Explain how it helps you to imagine better the original idea (here: a beach umbrella).

✎ *For practice*

Discuss the effectiveness of the following underlined images.

1. [As Rear-Admiral Tyndall looked at the Arctic convoy from the deck of *HMS Ulysses*], the squadron presented a fantastic picture now, <u>little toy-boats of sugar-icing, dazzling white</u>.

2 The water sparkled <u>as if sequins were dropping through it</u>.

3 Myriads of tiny fish were drifting through the water and he could feel the tiny touches of them against his limbs. It was <u>like swimming in flaked silver</u>.

4 He began swimming, over a middle region, where <u>rocks lay like discoloured monsters under the surface</u>, and then he was in the real sea.

5 The girl at the telephone switchboard was a skinny blonde with a strained, white face, <u>as if</u> <u>the black leech of the earphones had already drawn too much blood</u>.

6 As he went towards the lift, Blackwood glanced back at the desk and saw the desk clerk was watching him; <u>he had lifted the protective veil of indifference</u> for a moment and was peering out <u>like an old woman from behind a lace curtain</u>.

7 Blackwood did not answer. The silence stretched out <u>like scotch tape from a roll until there seemed no logical place to cut it</u>.

◆ Now copy and complete the table below to review your progress.

Progress review	Yes
I can identify similarities and differences between fiction and non-fiction.	
I can see how language has changed over the years.	
I can see how an author progresses an argument using various methods of linkage.	
I can identify techniques used to create suspense.	
I can distinguish between denotative and connotative uses of language.	
I can comment on the effect of a writer's use of imagery.	

Chapter 7
Biography and autobiography

Autobiographical writing is when someone tells the story of his or her own life, whereas in a biography, the story of a person's life is written by someone else. The main difference is that the autobiography will be told in the first person ('I') and will contain much about the person's feelings and thoughts as he or she looks back. By contrast, the biographer will rely on secondary sources – diaries, letters, reports, discussions with people who knew the person and so on.

Introspection and retrospection

The starting point in both a biography and an autobiography will obviously be to retell events that happened in the past, but there is much more to these genres than that. A key aspect is the element of reflection: the writer can look back on past events with the benefit of hindsight. The process of looking back is called **retrospection**.

However, the memory can be unreliable: often when someone revisits the scene of some past event it can seem different from how they remember it. It might even be that, as the playwright Harold Pinter wrote: 'There are some things one remembers even though they may never have happened.'

'Life must be lived forwards but can only be understood backwards.'

Danish philosopher Soren Kierkegaard (1813–55)

People's feelings about the past can also change with time, and the consequences of a past event can lead on to unexpected developments. What seemed a disaster at the time might have turned out to be the beginning of something new and positive. The process of looking inwards and examining your own thoughts, feelings and motives is called **introspection**.

Autobiography

You may have read some of Jacqueline Wilson's books. In this autobiographical article, she looks back on childhood picnics but discovers her memory is not always reliable.

Tuck in! Jacqueline Wilson's childhood picnics

The glorious picnics that the children's author Jacqueline Wilson recalled from the stories she had loved when young do not stand up to adult scrutiny. So, for her latest book, she made sure that she included some thoroughly foodie twenty-first-century feasts.

1   Flick through the pages of Enid Blyton's many hundreds of books and you'll find enthusiastic accounts of breakfasts, lunches and teas – and picnics a-plenty. Oh, how I loved reading about those picnics!

2   When I was growing up food rationing had only just stopped, and supermarkets hadn't yet started. Children ate plain bread and butter for tea, and even jam was considered a treat. In our household a bottle of Tizer was a Sunday extravagance, and we were allowed only one small glassful. Ask anyone to describe an Enid Blyton picnic and they'll mention lashings of ginger beer. I'd never tasted ginger beer, but it seemed as exotic and desirable as vintage champagne. I positively drooled when I read my way through the Famous Five books. No matter how dire the circumstances, the plucky quartet of children always managed to devour a wondrous picnic. Well, that's how I remember it.

3   I recently wandered into a Waterstone's and flicked my way through the series at random to find the special picnic parts. I wish I hadn't. I picked up *Five Run Away Together* and read that the Famous Five certainly drank ginger pop, needing it to wash down a peculiar picnic of tinned meat, then a tin of pineapple, and then a tin of sardines with biscuits. Maybe Timmy the dog wolfed it all down, but I'm surprised the four children weren't sick.

4   I tried to find other descriptions of the magnificent picnics I remembered in the books I had read as a child. I found the picnic passage in *Little Women*, and that proved disappointing, too. It says it was a hearty meal, but it doesn't describe it in any detail whatsoever.

5   But somehow or other books gave me a passion for picnics that wouldn't go away. Even the very word made my mouth water. We didn't often go for picnics as a family. We rarely went on any outings. We didn't have a car, and coach trips to the coast made me feel so travel sick I could only manage to suck barley sugar. However, every August my father would take a day off work and take me out into the Surrey countryside for a picnic.

6   I may have been a wimpy little kid, but I'd stride out determinedly in my Clarks school shoes, admiring the countryside and making up stories in my head. I'd start looking hopefully at my father's haversack 10 minutes after we set out. After half an hour I'd be ravenous, even if it was only mid-morning.

7   'When can we have the picnic, Dad? Can it be soon? Oh please, I'm starving!' I'd beg.

8   My father generally had a picnic spot in mind – and often it would be miles and miles away. That's why I loved to go to Oxshott Woods most of all. We didn't have far to walk. We had a gentle saunter through the beautiful woods, breathing in the smell of pine – then we were there, at the sandpit.

9   The sandpit seems to have shrunk now. Perhaps I've just got much bigger. When I was a child it seemed as vast as the Sahara, huge and yellow and satisfyingly steep, so you could run down it headlong or slide on your bottom. But that was fun reserved for after the picnic. That was the best bit and had to come first.

10   My father and I would search around for the comfiest spot, where he could lean against a tree, and I could take my shoes and socks off and dabble my feet in the hot sand. Then he'd slowly open the haversack and share out the picnic.

11   It wasn't elaborate. We had cheese sandwiches and a bag of tomatoes. Then we had banana sandwiches as a kind of pudding, occasionally sprinkled with sugar. Then we had a chocolate biscuit, a Penguin in a shiny wrapper, red or green or blue. Then we had an apple. We drank Rose's Lime Cordial from a flask. And it was bliss, sheer bliss, every single bite.

12   When I came to write *Four Children and It*, my tribute modern variation on E Nesbit's wonderful *Five Children and It*, I decided to rehome the Psammead, the cantankerous sand-fairy. He no longer resided in a gravel pit in Kent. He took up residence in the most magical place of my childhood, the sandpit in Oxshott Woods. Therefore my four children have to enjoy many picnics in Oxshott Woods, to speed the story along and enable the Psammead to grant them wishes (which of course nearly always go disastrously wrong).

13   I had such fun inventing those picnics. I knew modern children would not be particularly impressed with a few sandwiches and a chocolate biscuit. Alice, the children's stepmother, fancies herself as a domestic goddess. I knew she'd produce pretty spectacular picnics, different every day.

14   This is the first: 'We had bacon, lettuce and tomato sandwiches and cheese and tuna ciabattas and hard–boiled eggs sprinkled with salt with crisp toast triangles. There was an asparagus quiche, and little chipolatas and a vegetable dip. We had a blackberry-and-apple pie for pudding with Greek yogurt, and peaches and grapes and clementines.' I did wonder about lashings of ginger beer, but decided the children would prefer Coke and lemonade.

15   If it is promisingly sunny on publication day, I shall celebrate with an approximation of that picnic!

⊕ *Taking a closer look: the exploration of memories*

1   There are several words that could be used to describe Jacqueline Wilson's mood as she looks back on her childhood in this passage, such as:

- sentimental
- yearning
- nostalgic
- wistful.

These words all have similar meanings but with subtle differences. Copy and complete the table below and match words up to the definitions, using a dictionary if necessary.

Word	Meaning
	Looking back fondly at the past.
	Looking back fondly at the past, with a touch of regret or sadness.
	Looking back fondly at the past in an emotional way, 'through rose tinted glasses', making it seem more pleasant that it really was at the time.
	Looking back fondly at the past with a powerful desire to be able to go back to it, impractical though that is.

2 Choose the word that you feel most accurately describes the writer's mood. Write down TWO quotations from the passage to back up your answer.

3 When she looked back at the books she enjoyed as a child, Jacqueline Wilson felt rather disillusioned.

   a) What disappointed her when she reread the description of the picnic in *Five Run Away Together*?

   b) What disappointed her when she reread the description of the picnic in *Little Women*?

4 Look at paragraph 9.

   a) How does she view the sandpit now as an adult compared to her view of it as a child?

   b) Find a simile that describes the sandpit. How is this effective in emphasising what the sand seemed like to her as a child?

5 In paragraphs 5–11 she describes her memories of childhood picnics.

   a) Write down the main features of these picnics, and the aspects she liked about them. Simply stick to *facts* – don't include descriptions of feelings.

   b) Using the notes you have made, write a paragraph of no more than 100 words summarising the picnics.

6 Now think about her *feelings and memories* of the picnics. From paragraphs 5–11, write down all the words and phrases you can find that convey how positively she felt about these experiences. Here are two examples to start you off.

Quotation	Feeling that is being expressed
'even the very word made my mouth water'	sense of taste, enjoyment of food
'admiring the countryside'	

7 In paragraphs 12–15 Jacqueline Wilson talks about the book she has written.

   a) Write down some of the ways in which it is connected with her own childhood experiences.

   b) What changes did she make to her descriptions of picnics?

   c) Why did she do this?

⚙ *Tools of the trade: sentence structure*

Throughout this passage the writer skilfully varies her sentence structures and sentence lengths to achieve various effects.

1 Creating lists

Look at the description of Jacqueline Wilson's childhood picnic.

The main point is stated in a short sentence at the start: 'It wasn't elaborate'. A sentence that is then developed in detail in the rest of the paragraph is called a topic sentence.

The opening words of the sentences could not be simpler: 'We had' and 'Then we had', repeated three times. In each sentence an everyday food item is mentioned. The effect is to show that there was nothing elaborate about the content of the picnic.

'It wasn't elaborate. We had cheese sandwiches and a bag of tomatoes. Then we had banana sandwiches as a kind of pudding, occasionally sprinkled with sugar. Then we had a chocolate biscuit, a Penguin in a shiny wrapper, red or green or blue. Then we had an apple. We drank Rose's Lime Cordial from a flask. And it was bliss, sheer bliss, every single bite.'

The last sentence is a climax to the whole paragraph, again using repetition to stress the intense pleasure she derived from this simple picnic as a child.

Contrast this with the picnic as described in Jacqueline Wilson's novel:

'We had bacon, lettuce and tomato sandwiches and cheese and tuna ciabattas and hard-boiled eggs sprinkled with salt with crisp toast triangles. There was an asparagus quiche, and little chipolatas and a vegetable dip. We had a blackberry-and-apple pie for pudding with Greek yogurt, and peaches and grapes and clementines.'

Did you notice how many times the writer uses 'and'? This is probably something you have been told *not* to do! However, the effect here is to stress the sheer amount and variety of food on offer; there seems to be an endless sequence of one delicacy after another, in contrast to the simplicity of the earlier description.

2 Different sentence lengths

A good writer varies the lengths of the sentences. You may have noticed that Jacqueline Wilson sometimes uses long sentences and at other times uses short ones. Look, for example, at paragraph 3:

'I recently wandered into a Waterstone's and flicked my way through the series at random to find the special picnic parts. I wish I hadn't. I picked up *Five Run Away Together* and read that the Famous Five certainly drank ginger pop, needing it to wash down a peculiar picnic of tinned meat, then a tin of pineapple, and then a tin of sardines with biscuits. Maybe Timmy the dog wolfed it all down, but I'm surprised the four children weren't sick.'

- What is the shortest sentence in this paragraph?
- Why is a short sentence suitable for the point she is making in it?
- Imagine that sentence had been joined to the previous one by a conjunction (joining word) such as 'and' or 'but'. Why would that have been less effective?

Here is another example from the passage:

'Ask anyone to describe an Enid Blyton picnic and they'll mention lashings of ginger beer. I'd never tasted ginger beer, but it seemed as exotic and desirable as vintage champagne. I positively drooled when I read my way through the Famous Five books. No matter how dire the circumstances, the plucky quartet of children always managed to devour a wondrous picnic. Well, that's how I remember it.'

- What is the shortest sentence in this paragraph?
- Why is a short sentence suitable for the point Jacqueline Wilson is making in it?
- Imagine that sentence had been joined to the previous one by a conjunction (joining word) such as 'and' or 'but'. Why would that have been less effective?

✎ For practice

The extract below is taken from Charles Dickens' *A Christmas Carol* and describes a vision of a feast shown to the miserly Scrooge by one of the ghosts that visits him.

The moment Scrooge's hand was on the lock, a strange voice called him by his name, and bade him enter. He obeyed.

It was his own room. There was no doubt about that. But it had undergone a surprising transformation. The walls and ceiling were so hung with living green, that it looked a perfect grove; from every part of which, bright gleaming berries glistened. The crisp leaves of holly, mistletoe, and ivy reflected back the light, as if so many little mirrors had been scattered there; and such a mighty blaze went roaring up the chimney, as had been never known for many and many a winter season gone. Heaped up on the floor, to form a kind of throne, were turkeys, geese, game, poultry, great joints of meat, sucking-pigs, long wreaths of sausages, mince-pies, plum-puddings, barrels of oysters, red-hot chestnuts, cherry-cheeked apples, juicy oranges, luscious pears, immense twelfth-cakes, and seething bowls of punch, that made the chamber dim with their delicious steam.

◆ Working with a partner, go through this extract, noting where short sentences, long sentences and lists are used. Try to think why these particular structures are well suited to what is being said in each sentence.

Word games

Choose a word from the box below that fits each of the following definitions.

1 looking back fondly at the past

2 the story of someone's life, written by that person

3 the story of someone's life, written by another person

4 the process of looking back

5 the process of looking inwards and examining your thoughts, motives etc.

introspection	retrospection	biography	autobiography	nostalgia

☑ Taking it further

Try producing an autobiography of your own. Think about a period from your own past life and either write an account of it or talk about it to your class or group.

The idea is to use the techniques mentioned above, particularly **introspection** and **retrospection**. When retelling your experience, do not just consider *what* happened; think about how you felt at the time and how you now feel differently. (If any good ideas come out of this exercise, you might like to explore them further to produce a piece of personal writing for your folio.)

⬜ For discussion

We noted at the start of this chapter that **autobiography** is a person's story of his or her own life, while a **biographer** tells the story of someone else's life.

Think about which of these two genres is likely to be more **accurate** and why. You might expect **autobiography** to be the more accurate genre, since surely the writer must know the whole truth about him or herself. However, it is not that simple. Why might an **autobiography** be inaccurate? Consider these possible reasons and rank them in order of importance. The writer might:

● suppress things that would make him or her look bad

● invent or alter things to make him or her look good

● find it too painful or embarrassing to write about certain things

● be mistaken about certain things

● wish to avoid offending people by telling the whole truth

● have forgotten certain events, or remember them inaccurately

● try to make dull events more entertaining by making things up

● alter the facts to arouse sympathy or admiration in the reader.

'Truth for anyone is a very complex thing. For a writer, what you leave out says as much as those things you include … There are so many things we can't say, because they are too painful.'

Jeanette Winterson, poet and novelist

A good biographer will try to present the subject truthfully. However, a **biography** might also be inaccurate.

Consider the following reasons and rank them in order of importance:

- Source information may be incomplete: for example, letters and papers might have been lost or destroyed.

- Facts might have been forgotten or never recorded.

- Where facts are not available, the biographer may resort to guesswork that is wrong.

- The biographer may suggest the person had thoughts and feelings that they did not have.

- The biographer may include material that is not true to make the book more sensational or entertaining.

- A source used by the biographer might be inaccurate.

- The biographer might dislike the person or wish to discredit him or her.

- The biographer might wish to make the person seem better than he or she really was.

- The biographer might pretend to know more than he or she really does.

- A source might be fake, e.g. a forged document.

Might any of the reasons listed on page 68 for making **autobiography** inaccurate also apply in the case of **biography**?

This discussion will help you realise that there are many factors that might lead to either genre not being completely reliable.

Biography

A good biographer will always undertake very thorough research and also quote sources in footnotes so that these can be checked. They may have to guess certain things, but they will make it clear that they are guessing and only claim facts as definite if they have evidence. Any guesses should be logical and reasonable, given the facts.

One of the most eminent modern biographers is Claire Tomalin, who has produced several best-selling books on the lives of great writers such as Charles Dickens, Thomas Hardy and Jane Austen.

The following extract is taken from Claire Tomalin's biography of Jane Austen.

Claire Tomalin

A proposal of marriage

Jane Austen wrote novels in which love and marriage were major themes, but she herself never married. It is fairly certain that she fell in love at the age of 19 with a young Irishman of her own age, Tom Lefroy, but his family prevented him marrying Jane as she had no fortune. Seven years later, she did receive a proposal of marriage, from a man 5 years younger than herself.

1   [In November 1802, Jane and her sister Cassandra were invited by the Bigg sisters, Alethea and Catherine, to their home, Manydown, where the Austens had so often enjoyed themselves.]

2   The young women had much to talk about and were planning long cosy winter evenings together; the Bigg sisters may have had something else in mind as well. Their father was at home, a hale

sixty-year-old; so was their younger brother, Harris, who had [had his twenty-first birthday] in May. He had been away finishing his education at Worcester College, Oxford, so Jane and Cassandra had not seen him for some time; the shy, stammering boy, although still awkward in manner, had turned into a broad-shouldered, tall and much more confident young man. He was after all the heir to considerable estates.

Jane Austen

3 On the evening of 2nd December, Harris asked Jane to become his wife. It seems likely his sisters conspired with Cassandra for the couple to be left alone together, in the library, perhaps, or one of the small drawing rooms. It may also be that they had encouraged Harris to make his proposal; he was their little brother, and they may have felt he needed some help. Because of his stammer he had been privately educated at home until he went to Oxford, and the stammer still remained, which meant that social life could be something of an ordeal, and made him occasionally aggressive. So perhaps his loving and powerful elder sisters persuaded him that a wife he had known and liked all his life would solve his problems and make him a happy man. Whether Harris fancied himself in love with Jane or not, he decided she would make a good wife, and duly proposed.

4 Jane, no doubt very fond of her friends' brother, whom she would have danced with when he was a child, accepted his proposal. The discrepancy in their ages was only five years...The entire Manydown household was delighted. The evening was passed in congratulations, and everyone went to bed rejoicing. Jane would now become the future mistress of a large Hampshire house and estate, only a few miles from her birthplace, and close to her brother James... She would be able to ensure the comfort of her parents to the end of their days, and give a home to Cassandra. She would probably be in a position to help her brothers in their careers. She would be surrounded by dear sisters-in-law and friends. She would be a kindly mistress to the estate workers. She would have children of her own. All these thoughts must have rushed through her head, each one like a miracle, offerings of happiness she had given up expecting.

5 And she would have a perfectly decent husband. There she paused. Seven years before, she had danced here at Manydown with...Tom Lefroy... She had only to compare the emotions of that night with this one to realize what a gulf lay between real happiness and delusive dreams. The night went by, and Jane stayed awake, like a heroine in a novel who cannot sleep because too many emotions are pressing in on her... She thought and thought; and in the morning she packed her bag, dressed herself grimly, and sought someone – Alethea perhaps – who would find Harris. Again they were closeted alone in the library, or the small drawing room, and this time Jane explained, with all the delicacy in her power, that she had made a mistake and could not after all marry him...

6 After this, she and Cassandra could not stay on at Manydown as planned. Alethea and Catherine [Biggs] ordered the carriage and drove them home, where they all embraced tearfully by way of farewell...

7 To continue the story from Harris's point of view, he did not pine for long. Two years later he found a young woman from the Isle of Wight who could and did love him. They were married and she bore him ten children... On the face of it, the effects of the whole episode were no worse for Jane than for Harris. The friendship between the Austens and the Bigg sisters was undamaged. Harris moved away into a house of his own, and Jane was able to continue to visit Manydown as before. In fact, it marked a painful epoch in her life, because this was her last serious thought of marriage and the possibility of having children.

✛ *Taking a closer look: fact and conjecture*

Facts are pieces of definite information that can be cross-checked. For example, the biographer of a writer will know when the writer's books were written and published from publishers' records and reviews in magazines.

Conjecture (or guesswork) is where the biographer makes a reasonable assumption based on fact. If the writer had suddenly stopped producing books after the death of a family member, the biographer might reasonably assume that the writer had been emotionally traumatised by the death, even though there might not be direct evidence of this, such as a letter expressing grief.

1 **a)** Look at paragraphs 1 and 2. Pick out **four** definite facts that the author has researched and whose sources could be checked.

   b) From paragraph 2, pick out **one** piece of information that seems like guesswork or opinion on the part of the writer.

2 **a)** In paragraph 2, the writer suggests that Harris's sisters '*may*' have had 'something else in mind' when they invited Jane to their house.
   From paragraph 3, pick out **four** more expressions that make clear that she

is **guessing** at the role of the sisters in encouraging Harris to propose.

   b) How convincing do you find the writer's suggestions for the role of the sisters? Explain your reasons from the rest of the evidence in the first two paragraphs.

3 **a)** In paragraph 4, the writer thinks about Jane Austen's thoughts and feelings on the evening of the proposal.
   Pick out **two** expressions that make it clear that the author is having to *imagine* what these thoughts and feelings were.

   b) How convincing are the thoughts and feelings she attributes to Jane?

4 Look again at paragraphs 5 and 6. It is a recorded fact that Jane Austen accepted Harris Bigg's proposal on 2 December, but changed her mind next day.

   a) Pick out any **two** details given in these paragraphs that also seem to be definite facts.

   b) Do any of the details given in this section seem to have been imagined by the writer rather than researched as facts?

5 Look at the facts given in paragraph 7 about how the lives of Harris Bigg and Jane Austen developed after this incident.
   How do these facts suggest clues to the feelings of Harris and Jane about the proposal and its later rejection?

Word games

Choose a word from the box below that fits each of the following definitions.

1 healthy

2 imagined

3 difference/variation

4 false/deceiving

5 shut away

6 period of time

| fancied | epoch | hale | discrepancy | closeted | delusive |

◆ Now copy and complete the table below to review your progress.

Progress review	Yes
I can distinguish between biography and autobiography.	
I can identify the role of thoughts, feelings and the senses in autobiography.	
I appreciate the effects achieved by the use of different sentence structures and techniques such as lists.	
I can identify topic sentences in paragraphs.	
I know why autobiography may not always be completely accurate.	
I know why biography may not always be completely accurate.	
I can distinguish between fact and conjecture in biography.	

Part Two
Putting the skills into practice

Practice Paper 1

Scotland needs to clean up its tourism act

Journalist **Alan Taylor** suggests that the Scottish tourist industry needs to improve in several respects.

One cold and wintry night not so long ago I disembarked from a bus in Ullapool. It was more than an hour late which meant that I'd missed the last connection to Lochinver. When I pointed this out to the driver, he was as sympathetic as a traffic warden. The only balm he could offer was that 'there are worse places to be stranded in than Ullapool'.

5 Happily for me, this turned out to be true. As the heavens darkened and a Wagnerian growl announced the imminence of rain, I made my way to the Ceilidh Place where a room was soon found and a cheerful glass put in front of me.

When I relayed my experience of public transport to locals none reacted with surprise. Rather I got the impression that I would have had a better chance of reaching my destination had I travelled on a
10 sledge pulled by huskies.

Therein lie the polar points of Scottish tourism. On the one hand, there is the attitude of those who couldn't care less, who regard service as a synonym for servility, who treat customers as if they are something smelly stuck to their shoe. Meanwhile, there are those who take satisfaction from other people's pleasure, who embrace the 'Welcome to Scotland' slogan, who are enthusiastic ambassadors
15 for their country and will attempt to kill you with kindness.

I was reminded of my Ullapool sojourn by the fact that we are in the midst of Scottish Tourism Week, which has apparently been going since 2006. Where have I been all these years?

Its theme is 'competing for growth', a catchphrase as meaningless as it is fatuous. In order to achieve this there will be pow-wows in smart hotels, an 'industry dinner' and a soirée at Holyrood, at all of
20 which the importance of tourism to the Scottish economy, which is put at £11 billion, will doubtless be incanted and applauded. Please take my excuses as read.

As a constant tourist in my own country I have my own thoughts on how we may compete for growth, none of which, I hasten to say, is concerned with what Visit Scotland and the numerous other 'agencies' involved in the industry do or don't do.

25 First, and perhaps foremost, it is worth saying that standards have generally improved over the last few years. Bad service and bad manners, which used to be the norm, are today so unusual they are remarkable.

30 Gone, hopefully, are the days when one – that is, yours truly – could turn up thirsty, ravenous and exhausted at an inn in the Borders after a 20-mile hike only to be told it was your own fault for walking so far. Oh, and by the way, don't even think about ordering food. The kitchen closed two months ago when the chef ran off with the chambermaid.

Having said that, I was recently in a swanky hotel in Pitlochry where the barman seemed to think he was dispensing drinks from his personal cellar, so reluctant was he to serve guests.

35 If that anecdote is illustrative of anything it is that we are more likely to pass on instances of bad practice than we are to make recommendations. Hence the popularity of Trip Advisor and other websites devoted to detailing the good, the bad and the ugly in the tourist trade.

But while there will always be places that make Fawlty Towers seem like Gleneagles there is undoubtedly room for improvement which ought to be highlighted during Scottish Tourism Week.

Among the biggest beefs of the complainers is cleanliness. Is it too much to ask that showers are
40 fuzz-free, carpets swept and furniture dusted? In many establishments it would appear it is.

The same goes for the countryside, parts of which make a landfill site look tidy. Thus attractive hedgerows and rural byways are rendered hideous by deposits of rubbish. It is the same with trees, in many of which you can't spot nesting birds for rotting plastic bags.

This is not attractive to me or to tourists, many of whom are drawn to Scotland for its hitherto
45 glorious scenery. Have if you must your tourism week. But what's urgently needed to keep the foreign legions coming is a national spring clean.

From the *Herald*, March 2012

1 Look at paragraph 4 (lines 11–15). **In your own words**, summarise the two opposite attitudes that are shown towards tourists visiting Scotland. **4**

2 Look at paragraphs 1 and 2 (lines 1–7). Explain **in your own words** how the writer has himself experienced the two attitudes referred to in question 1. **4**

3 Comment on how the image 'he was as sympathetic as a traffic warden' (line 3) is effective in illustrating the point the writer is making about attitudes to tourists in Scotland. **3**

4 Basing your answer on paragraphs 5 and 6 (lines 16–21), show how the writer's use of language makes clear his thoughts and feelings about Scottish Tourism Week. **4**

5 Explain how paragraph 7 (lines 22–24) performs a linking function in the development of the argument of the passage. **4**

6 **In your own words**, explain the ways in which the writer thinks attitudes to visitors have improved in recent years. Base your answer on lines 25–27. **2**

7 Referring to the last four paragraphs of the article (lines 37–46), summarise the ways in which the writer believes Scotland needs to improve if it is to succeed as a tourist destination. **4**

8 One language feature that Alan Taylor uses in this article is **hyperbole** (exaggeration). From anywhere in the passage, quote one example of this technique and explain how it relates to the writer's purpose. **3**

9 Suggest **two** ways in which the title 'Scotland needs to clean up its tourism act' is an effective one in view of the content of the whole passage. **2**

Total: 30 marks

◆ Now copy and complete a progress review checklist for Practice Paper 1. See page 98.

Practice Paper 2

School's out: how Britain embraced the junior prom

Sally Williams examines the phenomenon of the school prom and discusses why it has become such an important event in young people's lives.

It is 11 am on a Thursday in mid-July and Lucy Holloway, 16, has an appointment at CC's Hair Salon in Rainham, Essex. Lucy has agonised for several weeks about her hair. Preceding her arrival at the salon's door were at least twenty phone calls with her best friend.

Lucy is getting ready for a special occasion that so far has cost about £500 (hair, evening dress, shoes,
5   clutch bag, nails, jewellery, spray-tan, limousine hire).

In effort and cost you might presume Lucy is getting married. In fact, it's more important than that. 'You can have as many weddings as you want, but you only get one prom,' she says.

Ten years ago we did not have school proms to mark the milestones of GCSEs and A-levels. We had end-of-term discos. Now elaborate 'passing out' celebrations have become a cultural phenomenon,
10   stoking passions and rivalries, and refashioning our sense of what a school party should be. More than 85 per cent of schools in Britain hold school proms, which range from no-frills dinners in school halls to tailor-made extravaganzas in five-star hotels.

Dr Caroline Schuster, a chartered psychologist, believes the appeal and the distinctive red-carpet look – long frocks and limousines – come not only from US sitcoms and soaps but also from a
15   world where schoolgirls measure themselves against film stars and supermodels. Proms, she says, are an incitement to celebrity-fantasy. 'It gives you the chance to become as near a celebrity as you can.'

The prom season is short: only four weeks from mid-June to mid-July. Yet the prom business was estimated to be worth about £80 million last year. The average cost was £244 per person, with one in ten spending more than £500 and two per cent splashing out more than £1,500, according to a
20   survey by Holiday Inn.

The industry now includes 'prom management' companies, websites providing a database and venues and the Prom Show, a promotional fair. The prom has also helped to transform the fortunes of Moss Bros. Two years ago, the company had losses of £2.8 million. Last year, the menswear chain was back in profit, thanks, in part, to its prom hire business.

*   *   *

25 By 6 pm, several 16-year-olds are standing in the magisterial surroundings of the Pavilion Suite at Orsett Hall. The unceasing rain hasn't dampened the excitement as the teenagers flood in to inspect the formally laid tables, helium balloons and glittery fairy lights. The prevailing smell is of hairspray and scent. Friends who normally wear shapeless uniforms and dirty trainers are transformed into exotic peacocks in huge-skirted ballgowns, teetering heels and heavy makeup.

30 I'm taken aback with the effort. This year's prom has involved weekly meetings since September of the prom committee, made up of students and teachers, who voted on the theme. Fairy tales, princes and princesses, the Diamond Jubilee and the Olympics were rejected in favour of Viva Las Vegas with its opportunities for casino glamour, although there is no question of gambling: only a magician, chocolate playing cards and helium balloons in the shape of hearts, clubs, diamonds and spades.

35 Every detail has been overseen by the head of year. She is a believer in the prom as a rite of passage, centring on fun, dressing up and shared history. 'This is a celebration of their time with us.' The principal of the school sees the prom more as a social opportunity, a chance to open up the mystical world of formal dining. 'There will be children who will never go to a formal function like this, so it is a lifetime experience for them. And for those who do find themselves moving in such circles, this will
40 mean they will have learnt how to cope with it.'

By 10 pm the dancing has started. 'It's coming to an end,' Lucy says of the prom and also of five years with five close friends. Only two will be at the same college as her next year. 'I love how you accepted me and didn't laugh over my obsessions,' writes one in Lucy's end-of-year book. 'How we shared books; how we managed to have endless conversations about random stuff.'

45 I leave six girls swaying on vertiginous heels, teetering on the edge of adulthood.

Condensed from an article in the *Telegraph Magazine*, 11 August 2012

1 The passage begins by concentrating in detail on one particular girl. Why do you think the writer decided to do this? **2**

2 Comment on one aspect of the sentence structure of lines 4–5 (paragraph 2), which helps to convey the importance of the event to Lucy. **2**

3 Explain how the writer uses the metaphor 'milestones' (line 8) to support her point about the significance of GCSE and A-level exams. **3**

4 **In your own words**, summarise the reasons why school proms appeal to young people, according to lines 13–16. **3**

5 Referring to lines 17–24, explain **three** ways in which the rise of the school prom has had economic benefits. **3**

6 Look at lines 25–29. Explain how the author uses contrasting word choice to emphasise how special the event is for the teenagers attending. **4**

7 Read lines 30–34. Identify the author's attitude to the planning of the event and give evidence to support your answer. **3**

8 With reference to lines 35–40, summarise **in your own words** the various ways in which the school staff consider the event to be of benefit to those involved. **6**

9 Comment on the image used in the final sentence (line 45) and explain how it is an effective way of bringing the passage to a conclusion. **4**

Total: 30 marks

◆ Now copy and complete a progress review checklist for Practice Paper 2. See page 98.

Practice Paper 3
The price of bacon

As food production becomes ever more technically advanced, concerns are being raised about the safety of some methods. In this article, **David Derbyshire** takes a closer look at one of Britain's favourite foods.

There is something irresistible about the smell of fried bacon. It's one of the delights of being a meat-eater and possibly the single most common reason why weak-willed vegetarians throw in the towel. For some, the joy of bacon lies in rashers squeezed between factory-sliced white bread and smeared with tomato ketchup. For others, it's the crisp slice of streaky bacon on the British breakfast plate,
5 ready to be dipped into a runny yellow yolk or a dollop of baked beans. And our love affair shows no sign of fading. A recent poll of Britain's best-loved 100 foods saw bacon at number one, beating chicken into second place and knocking chocolate into third. But while one in ten Britons claim bacon as their favourite, are those rashers that sizzle so seductively in the pan what they seem?

One problem may lie in a form of iron called *haem* that is found naturally in red meats such as beef, lamb
10 and pork. It can trigger the formation of substances called N-nitroso compounds (NOCs) in the body which can damage the lining of the bowel. Some types of NOCs have been linked to bowel cancer.

Another health risk comes from the salt, sodium nitrite and potassium nitrate which are added to bacon. These last two chemicals stop bacteria and keep the meat bright red so it looks fresh. However, nitrites and nitrates have also been shown to increase the risk of cancer in animals. Amid
15 such health fears, the British pig industry says it has cut down the level of potentially harmful additives. But there is a limit to how much can be reduced. 'If you go too far, it stops becoming a cured meat,' said a spokesman for the British Pig Association. 'Instead it's fresh meat and it doesn't keep so long.'

However, preservatives aren't the only dangerous additives in bacon. Traditional smoky bacon gets its distinctive taste by being hung over smouldering wood chips. You'd be forgiven for assuming that
20 smoked food – which has been eaten for thousands of years – is harmless. But some studies have shown that smoked foods contain cancer-causing compounds which are formed when wood burns, although the evidence linking smoked meats and cancer is not very strong.

Another problem is that cheap cuts are not treated with real smoke but are often sprayed with a 'natural liquid smoke extract' (made by condensing real smoke into a powder or liquid and mixing it
25 with water). When the European Food Safety Authority investigated 11 of these smoke extracts in 2010, it found that one could be harmful to people, while several were dangerously close to levels which may cause harm.

Perhaps the most surprising additive to bacon is water which is used to make rashers look bigger. The water is the reason why cheap rashers ooze so much white fluid in the frying pan – and then
30 shrink. Revealingly, a survey by the consumer magazine *Which?* found that rashers sold by leading supermarkets had more than 10 per cent added water.

Which? Also found that the labels which signal the bacon's country of origin are very misleading. Until supermarkets signed up to a new voluntary code, the practice was widespread to label as 'British' meat that had been raised in Holland or Germany because it had been cured in the UK. And this
35 issue raises another problem with your morning rasher. British pigs are among the best looked after

in the world. But less than 40 per cent of the pork we eat is British. The rest comes from countries where welfare standards are often appalling.

Meanwhile, the British Pig Association says shoppers should not worry about pig welfare in the UK and that 94 per cent of our farms are part of an assurance scheme that guarantees high standards of
40 welfare – from the size of pens to the amount of food and play material for pigs. Farms are inspected each year and get a vet visit at least four times a year.

But despite such attempts to reassure consumers, Compassion in World Farming says British intensively-reared pigs still suffer because most are housed indoors and do not get enough mental stimulation. With a lack of bedding or material to snuffle around in, pigs often turn aggressively on
45 each other. Although farmers are no longer meant to dock piglets' tails routinely, many continue to do so in order to prevent bite damage. And many piglets have their teeth ground down to stop biting – a procedure that can be painful. In the UK, new mothers are routinely confined in farrowing crates. The crates are designed to stop sows crushing their young. But unable to build a nest or move around the sows become frustrated and stressed, according to the RSPCA.

50 Amid all these welfare concerns, the best route for shoppers is to hunt down specialist bacons – the pricier dry cured rashers from organic or free range pigs. Of course these are more expensive. So when it comes to enjoying Britain's favourite food, there's a cost to your pocket if you want it guilt-free – and a cost to your health if you don't.

Adapted from an article in the *Daily Mail*, August 2012

1 Show how the writer engages the reader's attention in the opening paragraph (lines 1–8) by appealing to a number of the **senses**. Comment on the writer's word choice and support your answer with quotations. **4**

2 Choose **one** of the following images:
'weak-willed vegetarians throw in the towel' (line 2)
'our love affair shows no sign of fading' (lines 5–6)
'… bacon at number one, beating chicken into second place and knocking chocolate into third' (lines 6–7)
Explain fully why the image you have chosen is effective in expressing the writer's meaning. **3**

3 With close reference to the text, explain clearly how the last sentence in paragraph 1 ('But while one in ten … what they seem?') acts as a link in the structure of the writer's argument. **3**

4 Look at lines 9–11. With close reference to the text, explain how far the writer has convinced you that 'haem' is dangerous. **4**

5 In the next four paragraphs (lines 12–31), the writer looks at things that are sometimes added to produce bacon. **Using your own words as far as possible**, summarise these and their dangers. **6**

6 In the next section of the article (lines 32–49), the writer considers how pigs are reared and how humane their treatment is. He summarises the views of the British Pig Association and the Compassion in World Farming organisation. Which side of the argument do you feel the writer most favours? Clearly state your reasons, looking at:
a) the structure of the writer's argument, and
b) the writer's language and word choice. **6**

7 The title of the article is 'The price of bacon'. Think of the possible meanings implied by the title. Explain in some detail how it is appropriate for the passage as a whole. **4**
Total: 30 marks

◆ Now copy and complete a progress review checklist for Practice Paper 3. See page 98.

Practice Paper 4

Scotland's greatest cartoonist

The Dundee publisher DC Thomson recently withdrew *The Dandy* comic from publication after a drop in sales. In this article, journalist **John MacLeod** pays tribute to Dudley D Watkins, the comic's illustrator.

It is worth remembering the man for whose extraordinary talents the company expressly launched *The Dandy* in 1937 after the sensational impact of his new cartoon strips in its *Sunday Post*. Even as the clouds of war loomed, *The Broons* and *Oor Wullie* were already national institutions. Such was the brilliance of Dudley D Watkins that, of all the publisher's artists, he was one of only two in its empire
5   allowed to sign their strips.

And his characters, from Lord Snooty to Desperate Dan, and the varied worlds – touching or hilarious or bonkers – they inhabit delight us still. He is universally accepted as Scotland's greatest ever cartoonist. Thanks to his great range and astonishing draughtsmanship he is, even decades after his death, still remembered by the public. ('Aye, the guy who did the Broons.')

10   Yet he was Scottish neither by birth nor upbringing. Dudley D Watkins was born in Manchester in 1907 and was 18 when his family moved to Scotland. After a year at Glasgow School of Art, its principal personally recommended Watkins to the management at DC Thomson. Initially on a six-month contract, he was soon in Dundee, dashing off earnest illustrations for the publisher's papers for boys. Boasting titles such as *The Rover* and *The Hotspur*, these long-gone comics had boarding-school
15   romps and plucky young heroes aplenty. But so scant was his pay that Watkins in these early years had a side-line in teaching at Dundee Art School. In 1933, though, he was set, for the first time, to comic-strips, where bosses soon noticed his considerable flair.

Then, in March 1936, in chortling collaboration with editor R D Low, they cooked up characters for a new Fun Section in the *Sunday Post*; a wee lad with a bucket and a vast family in a tenement flat.
20   The rest is history. Watkins had soon created Desperate Dan for the new *Dandy*, one of the most enduring characters in an endearingly ridiculous milieu. This lantern-jawed cow pie-loving cowboy lives in Cactusville, a town with very British telephone boxes and irrefutably Dundonian! bobbies. The comic's sister paper, *The Beano*, was launched the following year and later still, new post-war titles – *The Beezer* and *The Topper* – which would last till the 1990s, added still more to his workload.

25   It was a burden he bore lightly. In fact, Watkins even drew strips for free. He was an earnest Christian – a pillar of the Church of Christ in Dundee – and over many years, drew for mission calendars without charge. He also penned comic strips in the *Young Warrior*, an evangelical publication for children, for which he took no payment either. Even at work, Watkins always had a huge Bible to hand, propped open on a sort of easel. He planned, one day, to draw a great illustrated Bible, no doubt in final happy
30   retirement. (He had blissfully married and built himself a fine big house in Broughty Ferry.)

The prevalent attitudes of his age, rather than his faith, were to blame for those aspects of his work that have not aged well, especially in his adventure-strips; too much of it now seems like racial caricature. But it should be stressed that he so detested the Nazis – and so frequently, and with

brilliance, caricatured them – that the Germans had Watkins listed, come conquest and occupation,
35 for early arrest.

On the larger, British stage, Watkins' formal adventure stories are naturally big on duty, courage and unassuming heroism. But two things leap out about his art itself. One is its enormous range. His formal illustrations for popular editions of such classics as *Robinson Crusoe* and *Treasure Island* are of such immediacy and gravitas that used copies sell today for large sums. But then you have the jaunty,
40 ridiculous exploits of Desperate Dan, drawn in an evidently more chucklesome hand, or the square-jawed teens of his adventure tales. Watkins had just one endearing blind spot, he could never quite draw a convincing cat (though his dogs are perfect in form and mischief).

The exploits of *The Broons*, though, must be his greatest achievement. That is partly because, deliberately, each storyline had fewer panels than *Oor Wullie*, allowing him to play with perspective
45 and tableau. He loved to get as many of the family into a single frame as possible. But apart from his perfect realisation of each of them, even incidental characters are wonderfully drawn, so much so that you can still recall a given battleaxe or auld grump, from a single story, decades later. And then there is the simple detail of scene – wifies windae-hangin' joyously the length of Glebe Street; the interior of local shops; the cosiness of the kitchen. *The Broons*, in particular, exemplifies the second truth of
50 Watkins' brilliance, a very deep tenderness. You laugh with the family, not at them. Their moments of genuine warmth – and there are many – are moving, not treacly.

When Watkins died so suddenly on August 20 1969 – his wife found him slumped over the latest artwork – *The Broons*, really, died with him. Much was soon successfully carried on by new, keen hands. But the *Desperate Dan* storylines were recycled in *The Dandy* for fully fourteen years before
55 Thomson's dared to set another artist about Cactusville. And the *Sunday Post* strips, likewise, were for years churned out from the archives. When new hands, of varied skill, assumed the stories, they were never the same again: the drawings flatter, the detail scantier, the characters somehow diminished, even colder.

Adapted from an article in the *Daily Mail*, August 2012

¹*Dundonian: from Dundee*

---

1 **In your own words**, briefly summarise **three** points made by the writer in the first paragraph which illustrate that Watkins' talent was already recognised as exceptional in 1937. **3**

2 **In your own words**, sum up the reasons given by the author in paragraph 2 (lines 6–9) for the enduring appeal of Watkins' work. **3**

3 ('Aye, the guy who did the Broons.') (line 9)
  a) Suggest a reason why the writer includes this comment.
  b) Comment on the writer's choice of language in this phrase and why it is effective. **3**

4 Explain the part played by the first sentence of paragraph 3 'Yet he was Scottish neither by birth nor upbringing' (line 10) in the structure of the writer's argument. **2**

5 Referring closely to the text, show what the writer's language in paragraph 4 (lines 18–24) reveals about Watkins' relationship with R D Low, the editor of the *Sunday Post*. **4**

6 a) The writer admits that the racial caricatures found in some of Watkins' strips are not acceptable today. Identify the reason why, according to the writer, Watkins drew such cartoons:
  i) he felt it supported the missionary work of his church
  ii) he was reflecting the attitudes held by society at the time
  iii) he was a racist due to his extreme Christian faith **1**

  b) Explain how the comments about Watkins and the Nazis in lines 32–34 develop our understanding of Watkins' true attitudes. **2**

7 '… two things leap out about his art itself' (line 37)

Explain fully **in your own words** the 'two things' discussed by the writer in the rest of the paragraph. **4**

8 Explain **in your own words** the evidence in the last paragraph which shows that the publisher DC Thomson found it almost impossible to replace Watkins after his death. **4**

9 Considering the article as a whole, sum up the main points the writer makes about the achievements of Dudley D Watkins. **Use your own words** as far as possible. **4**

Total: 30 marks

◆ Now copy and complete a progress review checklist for Practice Paper 4. See page 98.

Practice Paper 5
The end of the line

So many people now own mobile phones that landlines are being used less and less. In this article, **Ray Connolly** reflects on the change.

There are four contraptions of plastic and metal gathering dust around our house. There's one on my desk, another in the kitchen, a third in the sitting-room and a fourth by our bed. We used to call them telephones, but now they are better known as landlines – and they are remarkable only in that they hardly ever ring.

5 Actually, that's not quite true. Young men and women, who introduce themselves as Sally or Craig, call four or five times a week. Now, whenever I hear the familiar satellite hum and am asked if I am Mr Connelly, I simply reply, 'No, I'm afraid Mr Connelly is in jail,' which puts paid to any further conversation.

Of course, I'm not in jail. I'm in hiding from cold-calling[1] nuisances, and sitting here reminiscing about
10 the great days of the landline, that window of time before the whole developed world embraced the mobile and its successor the smartphone, and before email and texting replaced the spoken word.

I'm not saying this development is bad. Far from it, as I do my work almost entirely through email. And if it means that more people are now using the written word to communicate, thus confounding the Jeremiahs who told us that children wouldn't learn to write if they all had phones in their pockets,
15 it certainly has a plus side. But not many technological advances come without the odd regret. And with the continuing decline in the use of the landline with over 85 per cent of the adult population now owning a mobile, an era has almost gone for good.

Today, a mobile is considered an absolute necessity for every adult, and a vast majority of secondary school children have one. But I'm old enough to remember the days when relatively few people
20 even had a phone in their family home, when it was something big and black that sat in the doctor's surgery telling you how important a man he was. We didn't have a phone in our house until 1961, when I was 20, so if any calls had to be made it meant either cycling more than a mile to my mother's dress shop or taking four old pennies to the red telephone box near the bus stop. It would seem an awful chore now, especially on a wet November night.

25 But making those first teenage calls, with the ritual of the pennies being pushed into the slot, tremulous fingers carefully dialling the number, then the clanging of copper alloy on steel with the pressing of Button A when the receiver at the other end was picked up, was almost always exciting. You didn't make a phone call lightly in those days. Later, as a student, being able to speak to the object of your affection long distance, imagining her sitting in the chill of her parents' hall – because phones
30 always seemed to be kept in the coldest place in the house – was supreme. And, oh, the pain when the pips began and there was no more change to put in the box.

Not that romance governed everyone's early telephone experiences. Richard Branson has often told how, when starting out as a teenage record entrepreneur and living in an unconnected Notting Hill flat, he would take up residence in the phone box outside his window and use it as his office,
35 requesting that customers called him there. These days, if it were possible to find such a thing as a

handy phone box, anyone monopolising it – or even waiting outside for a call at a pre-arranged time as some of us once did – would probably be arrested on suspicion of being either a drug dealer or a terrorist.

40 Now that our smartphones come with cameras, radio, music and TV, as well as apps for novel reading, games, shopping and news, it's possible to forget those simpler times when the phone had but one function. Gone, too, is the relationship between caller and telephone operator. Telephone companies still employ operators in call centres. They're usually functional and polite. But back then there was a mystery and romance about the person in the job – the faceless Samaritan who would make the connection for you.

45 Chuck Berry even gave the directory inquiries operator a main role in one of his most famous songs – *Memphis Tennessee*. 'Long distance information, give me Memphis Tennessee, help me find the party trying to get in touch with me,' he sang, taking the voice of the father desperate to contact his six-year-old daughter. But could the same poignant song be written today in a world of increasingly disposable mobiles and easy, almost universal communication? It's difficult to imagine.

50 Nor are songs the only part of popular culture to have changed with the digital revolution. The good old landline used to play an important role in movies with love stories being built around missed calls. Remember? The heroine has just walked out of the door when the hero phones her – heartbreak ensues. Then there were the thrillers. Late at night the terrified heroine, alone in the house in a semi-diaphanous nightie, picks up the phone to call the police and realises that the line is dead. It's been 55 cut. The killer is already inside. And he's coming for her.

Wireless technology has wrecked all that. People communicate with each other all the time, if only by text. Now, I rarely use my landline. Knowing that I'm saving time for everyone when I email or text, I've began to feel as though I'm intruding when I occasionally consider making an old-fashioned phone-call just for the fun of it.

60 So here I sit and consider the state-of-the-art landline telephone on my desk that so rarely rings, and which I so rarely pick up to call anyone. Who could have predicted that the 21st-century digital explosion would have condemned what was once a shared centre of the family? Or that we'd now spend more time writing to our friends and relatives with emails and texts than we do speaking to them? Sad, isn't it?

Adapted from an article in the *Daily Mail*, August 2012

¹cold calling: uninvited telephone calls offering goods or services for sale

1 Look at the first paragraph (lines 1–4). With reference to the text, explain fully how the writer captures the interest of the reader. **4**

2 Look at lines 5–11. Explain clearly, with reference to the text, how the writer reveals his attitude to cold callers. **4**

3 Look again at the fourth paragraph (lines 12–17). **In your own words**, sum up the writer's feelings about the recent changes in wireless technology. **3**

4 Look again at lines 18–31. With reference to the text, **and using your own words**, show in detail how the writer helps us understand the importance of the telephone in years gone by. **6**

5 Explain what the anecdote about Richard Branson (lines 32–38) contributes to the passage. Refer to both the information it contains and how it adds to the reader's enjoyment. **3**

6 In line 43 the writer talks of the 'mystery and romance' of using the telephone in days gone by. **In your own words**, explain the evidence in lines 45–55 that the telephone helped provide 'mystery and romance' in popular culture such as songs and films. **3**

7 How does the writer use **sentence structure** effectively to convey meaning in lines 53–55 ('Late at night … coming for her.')? **3**

8 Look again at the title of the passage, and at the last two paragraphs (lines 56–end). With reference to the text, explain fully the feelings expressed by the writer about the changes in wireless technology. **4**

Total: 30 marks

◆ Now copy and complete a progress review checklist for Practice Paper 5. See page 98.

Practice Paper 6

Help! I've got incurable hoarder disorder

Possessions are gems so, asks **Christopher Middleton**, why would anyone throw away their treasured memories?

It may have come 40 years too late, but at last I've got a good reason to give my mother as to why I can't possibly tidy up my bedroom. I've got hoarder disorder.

Yes, not only does this newly identified condition have a neat, rhyming ring to it, but it demonstrates why my inability to throw out my football programmes, school exercise books, back issues of
5 *The Beano* and boxes of old Scalextric track is due not to laziness or messiness, but to a bona fide medical affliction.

Apparently, when I, and millions like me, am asked to undertake a clear-out of old possessions, it triggers what researchers describe as 'abnormal activity in the anterior cingulate cortex'.

This can be a very nasty thing, let me tell you. I well remember lying on my bed and rolling around
10 in a rage of hot tears, having been told to throw away my Subbuteo team of Coventry City players (because I had accidentally knelt on them, and snapped them all off at the legs).

There I was, being woundingly called a cry-baby by my brother, when all the time I was in the grip of what scientists at the Institute of Living, in Hartford, Connecticut, have discovered to be an inbuilt disability when it comes to 'decision-making and categorisation issues'. Vindication at last.

15 I am quite sure, however, that we hoarders will continue to be misunderstood and victimised, partly because of the throwaway society in which we now live. Hold on to a TV set that doesn't work, or rescue a slightly snagged sweater from the dustbin, and you are seen as the sort of person who might live in a burrow made of back issues of *The Spectator*.

Look back just a few hundred years, though, and you'll find that in Middle English and Old Norse,
20 the word 'hord' meant treasure. And to those of us who value our past, that's exactly what our old possessions are: gems, jewels and doubloons made not of crude, base metal, but of gossamer-winged memories.

This is what I constantly tell my wife, who has taken over the de-cluttering mantle from my mother. Time and again, I find myself having to rescue my prep school cricket cap from her unsympathetic
25 grip, or ferret around in the waste paper basket to retrieve the programme from our daughter's nativity play, circa 1996.

'Why do you keep these things?' she demands.

'So that I can remember them.'

'When?' she insists. 'When are you are going to look at them? They just live in a big heap.'

30 This is true, of course, and would be the one weak point of my argument, except that I have recently removed my stacked-up treasures to the shed. She still resents their presence. 'I know they're out there,' she complains, casting a nasty look towards the end of the garden.

Ah well, that's prejudice for you. But I can't understand why the hoarding indulged in by innocent citizens attracts so much more hatred than other similar, but less-discriminated-against activities.

35 Keep a scrapbook when you're little, for example, and your parents and teachers applaud your diligent documentation of daily life. Write a diary, and if you're Samuel Pepys, you bring enlightenment to generations not yet born. As for archivists, they make an entire living out of keeping things that people might want some day. Indeed, the nation pays millions of pounds each year to the professional hoarders who work at the British Library.

40 But when an individual like me simply wants to keep a harmless, if comprehensive, record of their life, domestic war breaks out.

At least we can now brandish this scientific report, proving that our inability to throw things away is a disorder in its own right. Even if a cure could be found, though, I wouldn't want it. No thanks; after all these years, I'm determined to hang on to my hoarding habit.

From an article in the *Daily Telegraph*, 8 August 2012

1 Look at lines 1–8. **In your own words**, explain the reasons why the writer likes the term 'hoarder disorder'. **4**

2 Show how the writer's use of language in lines 9–14 conveys his attitude to the idea that untidiness can be explained as a medical condition. **3**

3 Choose **one** example of the author's use of jargon from anywhere in the first five paragraphs (lines 1–14) and discuss its effect. **2**

4 Look at lines 19–22. Show how any **two** examples of the writer's use of language help the reader understand why hoarders place so much value on things they owned in the past. **4**

5 Read lines 27–32. **In your own words**, summarise the main points made by the author and his wife during their argument. **4**

6 In lines 35–39 the writer refers to three ways in which people keep written records of the past:

- childhood scrapbooks
- diaries
- archive material

Choose **two** of these and explain why they are considered to be worthwhile. **4**

7 Read the last paragraph (lines 42–44). In your own words, state the two main points the author is making here. **2**

8 Comment on the ideas and/or techniques used in the final sentence (lines 43–44) and show how these provide an effective conclusion to the passage. **3**

9 In several places throughout the passage, the writer refers to incidents, memories or possessions from his childhood. Choose any **two** examples and explain how these illustrate any aspect of his argument. **4**

Total: 30 marks

◆ Now copy and complete a progress review checklist for Practice Paper 6. See page 98.

Appendix I

Aspects of grammar and syntax

For the National 5 exam, you will be expected to show a knowledge of basic grammar and syntax. By 'grammar' we mean the system of rules used in a language, and 'syntax' (literally 'putting together') is how words are arranged.

A grasp of the correct technical terms will help you to answer questions that ask you to discuss a writer's language. The terms likely to be most useful are in **bold type**, and you should learn them.

Use this chapter for reference, and do the exercises if you feel unsure of your knowledge.

Units of language

Syllables

Words

Phrases

Clauses

Sentences

Paragraphs

Syllables

Syllables are the sounds that make up words, e.g. *blackboard* has two syllables.

Words of one syllable are called **monosyllables**, e.g. *black*. Writers use many one-syllable words when they are aiming for simplicity, whether formal or informal. Words with multiple syllables, **polysyllables**, are typical of complex, formal writing. They are frequently of Latin or Greek origin, e.g. *translucent*, *diagnostic*.

Words

All words belong to one of the eight 'parts of speech'.

1 Nouns

Nouns are naming words. These can be:

- common (physical things, e.g. *book*; *table*; *chair*)
- proper (indicate particular places, people etc., e.g. *Scotland*; *William*); they start with a capital letter
- collective (names of groups of things, e.g. *herd*; *swarm*; *flock*)
- abstract (non-physical things, e.g. *happiness*; *fear*)

2 Verbs

Verbs are doing words, e.g. *see, jump, run*. The words '*be*' and '*have*' are also verbs.

- Verb **tense** indicates the time of an action: past, present or future. In English, the usual tense for narrative is the **past tense**, but the **present tense** is sometimes used, particularly to build excitement. Present tense is used in commentaries.
- **Participles** are also parts of verbs. **Present participles** end in *–ing*, and are often worthy of comment. A number of present participles can create a lively, energetic tone.

3 Adjectives

Adjectives are describing words, e.g. *cold, big, black, white*.

4 Adverbs

Adverbs are modifiers of verbs, adjectives or other adverbs, e.g. *quickly, fiercely*. Most adverbs of manner end in *–ly*, but many other types do not: *soon, tomorrow, now, then, therefore, however, very, not, never*.

Both adjectives and adverbs can be compared, in forms called: **positive** – **comparative** – **superlative**, e.g. *big – bigger – biggest*; *thoughtful – more thoughtful – most thoughtful*.

Superlatives are used frequently in the language of advertising, or in creating a dramatic tone, and are often worthy of special comment.

5 Prepositions

Prepositions may indicate position and introduce phrases. They are simple little words such as *in, on, under, before, after, by*.

6 Pronouns

Pronouns can take the place of nouns: *he, she, it, they* etc.

7 Conjunctions

Conjunctions are joining words, such as *and, but, or, since, because*. They are important in discussing linkage and sentence structure. The use of the word *and* is often particularly worthy of comment.

8 Articles

There are only three words in this category: *the* is known as the **definite article**; *a* and *an* are the **indefinite articles**.

Phrases

A **phrase** is a short group of words that forms a unit. Phrases can be noun, adjectival, adverbial or verb, e.g.

- noun phrase: *a large, blue car*
- adjectival phrase: *with a scar on his cheek*
- adverbial phrase: *tomorrow morning*
- verb phrase: *owned up*

Noun, adjectival and adverbial phrases are largely **descriptive**. A writer may use a large number of them in one sentence to build up tension, or to create a mood.

Clauses

A clause is a group of words that contains a verb, e.g.

a) 'The match **started** at one o'clock.'

b) 'Before he **left** the house …'; '… because she **disliked** swimming'.

Example (a) can stand alone and is known as a **principal clause**. The examples in (b) cannot stand alone and are known as **subordinate clauses**.

Sentences

A sentence is a group of words that makes complete sense. A **simple sentence** consists of one clause, e.g. 'The cat ran across the road.'

A **complex sentence** contains several clauses, e.g. 'When the dog appeared, the cat ran across the road, which was full of traffic at the time.'

Sentences can take several forms:

● **Statement**, e.g. 'The referee stopped the match.' Ends with a full stop.

> Since statements are the usual form of sentences, you need only comment on sentences that are *not* statements.

● **Command**, e.g. 'Stop the match!' Ends with a full stop or exclamation mark.

● **Exclamation**, e.g. 'What an amazing match it was!' Ends with an exclamation mark.

● **Question**, e.g. 'Was it a good match?' Ends with a question mark.

● **Rhetorical question**, e.g. 'Was the referee blind?' Although rhetorical questions end with a question mark, they do not expect an answer, and have a similar function to an exclamation.

● **Minor sentence**, e.g. 'A match I'll never forget.' A minor sentence has no main verb, but makes sense by itself. It can take the form of a statement, exclamation or question.

Sentence patterns

When you are asked to discuss sentence structure, you should also look for certain patterns. Some common ones are:

List

A writer will list a number of words, phrases or ideas. When you notice a list, look also for **climax**. A **climax** is a building up in importance. Very often items in a list show a **progression** of some sort.

Varied sentence lengths

Putting in short sentences often racks up tension, as the short sentences stand out from the longer ones.

Repetition

This may be of single words, phrases or sentence types. For example, you may notice several questions one after another.

Unusual word order

Certain positions in a sentence carry more emphasis than others. The most emphatic is the end of the sentence. If an idea is delayed until the end, this places special stress on it. This technique is known as **inversion**, e.g. 'Round the corner, in a shower of spray, rushed an ambulance.' If the phrase 'an ambulance' came first in the sentence, as you might expect, the effect would be less dramatic.

Parenthesis

Parenthesis is an extra piece of information added to a sentence, marked off by a pair of dashes or (less commonly) a pair of brackets. The sentence will still make sense if it is omitted. The extra information might be a comment, an example, an explanation, or a piece of description, among other things, and it may take the form of a single word, a phrase or a sentence. For example, 'Round the corner, in a shower of spray – it had been raining heavily that day – rushed an ambulance.' Here, the parenthesis gives an explanation for the spray.

If the parenthesis comes at the *end* of a sentence, a full stop, question mark or exclamation mark will be used instead of the second dash.

Paragraphs

In a piece of writing, sentences are grouped into paragraphs, each of which will be a stage in a story or argument. The first sentence is often a **topic sentence**, which introduces the subject, or 'topic', of the paragraph. The rest of the paragraph will then develop the topic.

Good writers will link paragraphs by including a reference to the paragraph that comes before it, or by using a linking word or phrase indicating the direction the argument is going, such as 'however' or 'moreover'. Older and more formal texts tend to have longer paragraphs than more modern or informal ones. A very short paragraph may be used to create drama.

Practice exercises

1 Identify the nouns in the following extract. Say what type of noun each is.

A clock in the schoolroom now struck; Miller left her circle and cried, 'Silence! Go to your seats!'

Discipline prevailed; in five minutes the confused group of girls was resolved into order, and there was comparative silence. The teachers stood in front; ranged on benches the eighty girls sat motionless.

2 Identify which **part of speech** each of the underlined words is in the following extract.

The servants brought in bread and cheese and distributed it to the girls. Then the order was given, 'Go to the garden!' Each put on a coarse straw bonnet, and a cloak of grey wool. The garden was a wide enclosure with high walls and a covered verandah down one side. A middle space was divided into little beds. When full of flowers they would doubtless look pretty; but now, at the end of January, all was brown decay. I shuddered miserably as I stood. The stronger girls ran about, but the thin and pale ones stood in a herd together in the verandah.

3 Try to decide which of the following underlined pieces of language are phrases, clauses or sentences.

On the morning of 5th December, the convoy left for Russia. Twenty merchant ships, laden with war supplies, were accompanied by four Royal Navy warships. Before long, the wind rose, and before they could change course, the ships were engulfed in a blizzard. The larger ships, which were well ballasted, rode the storm well, but the smaller ones were tossed unmercifully. The danger of collision was great.

4 a) All five of the **sentence types** explained above are to be found in the following extract. Can you identify examples of all of them?

b) How many of the **sentence patterns** described above can you find?

On an upright chair by a round table sat the owner of the house, Miss Lawson. She, too, had red eyes. Her hair was even untidier than usual. Dr Donaldson sat directly facing Poirot. His face was quite expressionless.

My interest quickened as I looked at each face in turn.

In the course of my association with Poirot I had assisted at many such a scene. A little company of people, all outwardly composed, with well-bred masks for faces. And I had seen Poirot strip the mask from one face and show it for what it was – *the face of a killer!*

Yes, there was no doubt of it. *One of these people was a murderer!* But which? Even now I was not sure.

'I protest,' Miss Lawson tossed her head angrily. 'Disgraceful, that's what it is! Disgraceful!'

'Be patient, mademoiselle,' said Poirot. 'Be kind enough not to interrupt.'

Punctuation

Punctuation marks are important as they are the keys to working out sentence structure.

1 A **full stop** ends a sentence that is a statement.
2 An **ellipsis** (…) is a row of three full stops. It is used to indicate something is being left unsaid. It can be used for humorous or dramatic effect.
3 A **comma** separates a subordinate clause or a phrase from the rest of a sentence. Commas are also used to separate items in a list, particularly if these are single words or very short phrases. If the items are longer, semi-colons are sometimes used instead.
4 An **exclamation mark**, as the name implies, marks an exclamation. Note that sometimes it is an indicator of tone – it may indicate surprise, horror, shock, amazement and so on. It can even be used ironically.
5 A **question mark** indicates a question, both simple questions and rhetorical questions. It is important to check if an answer is implied or not – it is a common mistake to think all questions are rhetorical.
6 A **semi-colon** (;) usually marks the end of a statement, but less strongly than a full stop. It may come between two closely connected statements. Semi-colons are also frequently used to separate items in a list.
7 A **colon** (:) usually follows a statement, and introduces some additional information, such as an explanation, an example, a list or a quotation.
8 A **dash** (–) can be used just like a colon to introduce additional information. A **pair of dashes** is the usual way to enclose a parenthesis. A dash is also used if a sentence is broken off suddenly – this is particularly common in direct speech, if a speaker is interrupted. In printing, a dash is a longer mark than a hyphen.

9 A **hyphen** (-) is used to link words to produce a compound noun such as *six-year-old*. In printing it can be used at the end of a line to split the syllables of a long word that cannot be completely fitted in. When printed, it is only half as long as a dash.

10 A **pair of brackets** may be used to mark a parenthesis. The second bracket is always used to close the parenthesis, even if it is at the end of a sentence.

11 An **apostrophe** (') marks possession (*Susan's book; the players' entrance*) or a missing letter in an abbreviation (*wasn't*). Apostrophes should never be used in simple plurals; this error is often known as the 'greengrocer's apostrophe'.

12 **Inverted commas** are used to indicate a quotation or direct speech when a conversation is written down.

The 'greengrocer's apostrophe'

✒ *For practice*

Punctuation marks have been omitted in the following piece of writing. Can you suggest which marks would make it easier to understand? You will also have to add some capital letters.

Bypassing picturesque farm houses and quaint villages the river Neckar ran towards its confluence with the Rhine between lush meadows here rich with wild flowers there dotted with black and white cattle along it constantly steamed big, black barges how we wished we could live on one of those laden with coal, gravel and other more mysterious things concealed under tarpaulins the barges were often gaily decorated with pots of red geraniums and a car would sit jauntily on board behind the wheelhouse often quite a smart car a Mercedes or an Audi who were those lucky people who made their living in such a delightfully way on the way to the Rhine was the magical city of Heidelberg home of The Student Prince a romantic red castle and at that time hordes of American soldiers.

◆ Now copy and complete the table below to review your knowledge of grammar and syntax.

Knowledge about grammar and syntax	Yes
I can recognise the six basic units of language: syllable, word, phrase, clause, sentence and paragraph.	
I can recognise common sentence patterns: list, variation in length, repetition, unusual word order such as inversion and parenthesis.	
I can identify the eight parts of speech: noun, verb, adjective, adverb, pronoun, preposition, conjunction and article.	
I can identify four types of noun.	
I can identify different tenses of verbs and present participles.	
I can identify degrees of comparison (comparative and superlative) in adjectives and adverbs.	
I am familiar with the functions of twelve types of punctuation mark: full stop, ellipsis, comma, exclamation mark, question mark, semi-colon, colon, dash, hyphen, brackets, apostrophe and inverted commas.	

Appendix 2
Glossary

alliteration: figure of speech in which there is repetition of initial and sometimes internal consonant sounds in a phrase, e.g. 'poppy pepper-pots'.

ambiguous: having two meanings, e.g. 'The cannibal liked children.'

anecdote: a small story, often personal, included to illustrate an idea in a larger piece of work.

anti-climax: a sudden falling off at the end of a list that builds up in rank or significance; a sudden relaxation of tension.

archaic: old-fashioned word or expression, e.g. 'thou' for 'you'.

atmosphere: creation of mood, often through senses, e.g. cold, damp.

characterisation: the creation and presentation of characters (people) in a text.

climax: the culminating point in a list of things that builds in significance; the peak of tension.

colloquial: the language of everyday speech. Includes abbreviations, e.g. 'can't'; informal expressions, e.g. 'dad' instead of 'father'; interjections such as 'well', 'of course', 'you see'.

connotation: associations of a word, or something associated with it, e.g. 'ash' and 'dust' have connotations of death, arising from phrases 'ashes to ashes, dust to dust' in funeral services; the colour red is associated with danger.

context: the immediate surroundings of a word or phrase; or the precise place in which it is used.

dialect: type of language used in a geographical area, e.g. 'lassie' is Scots for girl, 'bonnie' for pretty, 'burn' for stream. (Note: dialect is *not* slang.)

diction: word choice; words selected by a poet or writer.

emotive: describes language that expresses the writer's emotions and aims to arouse emotion in the reader.

euphemism: a gentler way of expressing something unpleasant, e.g. 'passed away' rather than 'died'.

expression: 'an expression' means a word, or, more usually, a phrase; 'expression' means style of writing.

extended metaphor: see metaphor.

figurative language: alternative for metaphor; describes speech that contrasts with literal (actual) meaning.

figure of speech: general term for language techniques such as simile, metaphor, hyperbole, alliteration, oxymoron and irony.

first person: using 'I', 'we', 'me', 'us' instead of 'he', 'they' etc.

flashback: a technique of structure where events move back to an earlier time.

genre: type of literature, such as poetry, drama, prose; or a subdivision of this, e.g. science fiction, thriller, detective story, narrative poetry.

hyperbole: exaggeration for dramatic or humorous effect

illustration: a detailed example or a small story that acts as an example.

image: an unlike thing something else is compared to, which will have one or more points of similarity. In the expression, 'the soldier was as brave as a lion', the image is 'lion', a fierce animal.

imagery: images used in similes and metaphors.

inversion: word order that places the verb before the subject or otherwise 'inverts' the usual word order of a sentence. This places emphasis on the word that is out of order, e.g. 'down she went'.

irony: saying the opposite of what you really mean for humorous effect or mockery; a twist of fate in events, such as an unexpected coincidence.

jargon: technical language or language that is used by specialists of some kind.

juxtaposition: placing one thing beside another to create an effect, such as contrast.

linear structure: events in a text take place in order of time.

link: a sentence (or sentences) that both refers to the idea just discussed and introduces the next one; any joining device in an argument, such as a conjunction.

metaphor: a comparison where one thing is said to *be* another; a comparison without using 'like' or 'as'. An **extended metaphor** is a series of images in which the same comparison is sustained.

minor sentence: a sentence in which the verb is omitted, as understood.

monosyllable: word of one syllable.

mood: the emotional feeling created in a piece of writing, e.g. tense, cheerful.

onomatopoeia: figure of speech in which the sound of a word imitates its sense, e.g. 'sizzle'.

oxymoron: a figure of speech containing an apparent contradiction, e.g. 'sweet sorrow'.

paradox: an apparent contradiction of ideas, e.g. 'you must be cruel to be kind'.

parenthesis: a word, phrase or sentence inserted into a sentence, giving extra information.

persona: a personality adopted by a writer, usually writing in the first person, which is not necessarily the same as the writer himself. For example, in *My Last Duchess*, Browning adopts the persona of a murderous duke.

personal: writing that refers to the writer's own experience and feelings, often in the first person; the personality of the writer will be clearly evident (in the case of impersonal writing, the opposite will apply).

personification: an inanimate object is spoken of as if it is alive, or has a mind of its own.

register: a form of language used in restricted circumstances, e.g. legal language, medical terminology.

rhetorical question: a question that does not expect an answer as the answer is assumed or seems obvious.

second person: use of the pronoun 'you' (both singular and plural).

sentence structure: types of sentence (statement, question, command, exclamation and minor sentence); word order, and the arrangement of phrases and clauses within a sentence.

setting: where and when the action of a text takes place.

simile: a figure of speech comparing two basically unlike things using 'like' or 'as'.

slang: colloquial expression that is unacceptable in formal language, e.g. 'loads of stuff' instead of 'many things'. Slang is often particular to an age group or period of time.

structure: the way a text is put together, e.g. using flashbacks; the development of ideas in an argument or stages in a story.

symbolism: additional meaning or significance of an object beyond the literal, e.g. darkness might be a symbol of evil or a clock might be a symbol of time passing.

syntax: the arrangement of words and phrases in a sentence.

theme: a main idea of a text.

third person: use of 'he', 'she', 'it', 'they' as opposed to 'I', 'we' (first person) or 'you' (second person).

tone: the expression of the writer's feelings or attitude to his subject, e.g. humorous, sarcastic.

word choice: writer's preference of certain words over others that have similar meanings.

Appendix 3

Sources of genre extracts

The sources for the twelve extracts in chapter 2 are as follows:

1 News report from the *Daily Telegraph*
2 *Dumb Witness* by Agatha Christie

    A classic crime novel featuring the Belgian detective, Hercule Poirot. First published in 1937, this novel is one of a long list of books featuring Poirot, which have again become popular following the successful television series featuring David Suchet as Poirot.

3 *Psychology for Higher: The Textbook for Psychology* by Gail Staddon, Aileen Duffy and Richard Cherrie

    Although intended for senior school students, this is also an interesting introduction to psychology for the general reader.

4 *Shooting an Elephant*, an essay by George Orwell

    First published in 1936. *Orwell* describes his experiences as a policeman in Burma in the days when it was part of the British Empire.

5 Film column from the *Metro* by Larushka Ivan-Zadeh

    Review of the film *The Bourne Legacy*, a follow-up to the highly successful Bourne Trilogy.

6 *Puss in Boots*

    A traditional fairy tale, originally taken from a book published in France in 1697. Written by Charles Perrault, the title of the collection of stories was *Tales from Times Past*, showing that even then the story was old.

7 Article from the Life section of *Metro*

    Alice Wiseman recommends a Turkish holiday resort.

8 *The Demon Lord* by Peter Morwood

    This is the second in the fantasy series 'The Book of Years', which is set in a kingdom called Alba. Morwood also writes science fiction.

9 *To the Bitter End*: *The Diaries of Victor Klemperer 1942–45*

    Translated by Martin Chalmers, this is the second volume of Klemperer's diaries. The first volume, *I Shall Bear Witness*, describes the years 1933–41. Klemperer was a professor at the University of Dresden. As a Jew he was the victim of Nazi persecution, but avoided immediate arrest as his wife was not Jewish. Klemperer survived the war, ironically thanks to the devastating Allied bombing in February 1945. In the resulting fire storm, many records were destroyed which enabled him to conceal his Jewish identity and mingle with German refugees.

10 *A History of the Scottish People,* 1560–1830 by T. C. Smout

    Written by a professor of history at the University of St Andrews, this is a scholarly but very readable account of Scotland's history.

11 *The Secret Power of Beauty* by John Armstrong

    An investigation into the question of how beauty can be defined and where it can be found.

12 *Buddha Da* by Anne Donovan

    A comic novel written in Glaswegian dialect, *Buddha Da* tells the story of Jimmy, who decides to become a Buddhist, and the impact this has on his wife and daughter.

Appendix 4

Practice Paper progress review

Progress review: Practice Paper _____	Yes
My answers were an appropriate length for the number of marks available.	
I used my own words in summary questions and questions on ideas.	
I gave evidence (quotations or close textual reference) to support my opinions.	
I quoted appropriate examples in questions on language and language techniques.	
Areas I must practise: *(underline as appropriate)*	
summary of main ideas; language techniques; tone; sentence structure; personal response	

The Publishers would like to thank the following for permission to reproduce copyright material:

Photo credits

p.v © Moviestore Collection/Rex Features; p.1 © Image Source/Getty Images p.4 © Hemeroskopion – Fotolia.com; p.8 © Ange / Alamy; p.9 © KtD – Fotolia.com; p.10 © NILS JORGENSEN/Rex Features; p.11 The Doric Columns (http://www.mcjazz.f2s.com/index.htm); p.13 © 2009, Hilary Mantell / Harper Collins Publishers; p.15 © Hodder Gibson; p.16 © The Sun / News Syndication; p.18 (top) © Doruk Sikman – Fotolia.com, (bottom) © Mary Evans Picture Library; p.19 © Blue Lantern Studio/Corbis; p.20 © INTERFOTO / Alamy; p.21 © Carl Simmons/ Rex Features; p.24 © PhotoEdit / Alamy; p.25 © Christopher Dodge – Fotolia.com; p.32 © c.Col Pics/Everett/Rex Features; p.33 © James Curley/Rex Features; p.37 © Getty Images; p.42 (top) © Radoslaw Korga – Fotolia.com, (bottom) © Octopus Publishing Group; pp.43-44 (all) © Octopus Publishing Group; p.46 (top left to right) © Imagestate Media (John Foxx) / Business Funnies SS145, © Image Source/Getty Images / Grad Class IS925, © Imagestate Media (John Foxx) / CEO SS137, © George Doyle/Stockbyte/ Photolibrary Group Ltd/ Big Business SD101, (bottom left to right) © Kevin Peterson/Photodisc/Getty Images/ Everyday People 2 CD 33, © Scott Griessel – Fotolia.com, © fasphotographic - Fotolia.com, © Gelpi – Fotolia.com; p.50 © PA Photos / TopFoto; p.51 © Holmes Garden Photos / Alamy; p.52 © Vanessa Mitchell, The Cage; p.54 © London Stereoscopic Company / Getty Images; p.55 (top) © Tierfotoagentur / Alamy, (bottom) © William Morris / Getty Images; p.56 © Mary Evans/Peter Higginbotham Collection; p.58 (top) © The Granger Collection / TopFoto, (bottom) © 2000 Credit:Topham / AP; p.59 © petographer / Alamy; p.60 © Imagestate Media (John Foxx) / Medicine & Healthcare Today 2 SS31; p.61 (left) © Francesco Carta Reportage / Alamy, (right) © 1997 Greg Kuchik/Photodisc/ Getty Images/ Eat, Drink, Dine 48; p.63 © The Granger Collection / TopFoto; p.64 © Bon Appetit / Alamy; p.68 © MYKEL NICOLAOU/Rex Features; p.69 © Geraint Lewis/Rex Features; p.70 © traveler1116 / Getty Images; p.73 © OJO Images Ltd / Alamy; p.93 © Smileus – Fotolia.com.